Young Britain

Young Britain

Politics, pleasures
and
predicaments

Jonathan Rutherford

Lawrence & Wishart
LONDON

Lawrence & Wishart Limited
99a Wallis Road
London E9 5LN

First published 1998

British Library Cataloguing in Publication data.
A catalogue record for this book is available from the
British Library.

ISBN 0 85315 867 3

Typeset in North Wales by
Derek Doyle & Associates, Mold, Flintshire.
Printed and bound in Great Britain by
Redwood Books Ltd, Trowbridge.

Contents

Introduction
Jonathan Rutherford   7

The us generation
Frances O'Grady   31

Underworked and underpaid
Ian Brinkley   39

A new deal for young black Britain
Balbir Chatrik   51

Bypassing politics? A critical look at DiY culture
Peter Gartside   58

Hijabs in our midst
Noshin Ahmad   74

Paradigm lost? Youth and pop
Rupa Huq   83

Ecstasy in the unhappy society
Jonathan Keane   98

'That's entertainment . . .': generation X in the time of
New Labour
Michael Kenny   112

Not such tolerant times
Bilkis Malek   127

Reading identity: young Black British men
Elaine Pennicott   147

The benefits of work?: lone motherhood under New Labour
Karen Triggs   154

Notes on contributors   168

Introduction

Jonathan Rutherford

Living in a new, old country

A sense of loss

On Saturday 6 September 1997, I walked onto Horseguards' Parade in London with my son. Thousands of people sat alone and in groups, listening to *Libera me*, an aria from Verdi's *Requiem*. Loudspeakers had been installed at strategic points around Westminster Abbey, and the melancholic sound of the soprano's voice lifted and swam across the open space. It felt as if the whole of London was still, contemplating in silence the loss of something intangible but crucial to our identities. Of all the political demonstrations I have been on – the public displays of hope, anger, bitterness and protest – none has succeeded in carrying the demotic, emotional power of Diana's funeral. During that bizarre and disturbing week of national mourning I found my republican disdain for royalty undermined by my own feelings of loss. Wandering around Kensington Palace and then down through Hyde Park to Buckingham Palace and the Mall was a type of minor pilgrimage. A population had been mobilised in an unprecedented display of public grief; a revolution of mourning at the passing of goodness and love. There was no patriotic rhetoric or regalia. The letters of condolence, the messages of empathy and the whimsical poems of bereavement carried their own protest at a failing royalty, and they did so in a manner that was pre-democratic in character. The instrumental and rational business of democracy had been swept away by an emotional religiosity. The country – the southern part of it at least – appeared to have succumbed to feudalism. We were all peasants again, the mob in a

Shakespeare play, our reason suspended, and our feelings swayed by one aristocrat or another in the internecine feuding for power.

What was it we were mourning? Our own dead mothers, fathers and grandparents? The loss of a sense of national belonging? An inexplicable grief for ourselves? Diana embodied a national desire to be vibrant, modern, pluralist and democratic. It was an ambiguous desire, compromised by her wealth and by her need for social status. Diana was dependent on the protocol and old fashioned values of the hereditary class she reacted against. Without them her iconic status as victim and rebel would have been meaningless. She helped to perpetuate what she professed to loathe. In her ambivalence she symbolised England's quandary over its relationship to its imperial and chauvinistic past. Diana wanted privacy even as she clung to fame and public adulation. She was a contradiction, because she was a transitional figure; she emerged out of Britain's archaic class system to become a symbol of a more cosmopolitan, tolerant and inclusive society. She could never have realised this future because she was a part of the problem. Standing in the square on the day of her funeral I imagined that this extraordinary period of mourning might signal a release from our national equivocation with class deference. As I waited with the crowds on the Mall for the hearse, expecting the pomp and circumstance of a parade of cars, even a mounted guard, I was caught unawares by a single hearse gliding silently past. Was this the long, historical contract between the monarchy and its people passing into history? In the traffic-free serenity of London, I felt a sense of liberation, as if, for a fleeting moment, the crowds owned the city.

Some months after the funeral I went to the *Sensation* exhibition at the Royal Academy. Here in the hallowed portals of the English arts establishment, young British conceptual art thumbed its nose at the refined taste of aesthetic convention. The twin motifs of conceptualism – new and shocking – were epitomised by Damien Hirst's famous preserved shark. In a gallery, out of bounds to people under eighteen years of age, stood Jake and Dinos Chapman's ring of child mannequins. They were naked and wore identical Fila trainers, their faces protruding with penises and indented with anuses and vaginas. The artists coyly evade accusations of paedophile abuse by entitling the piece *Zygotic acceleration, biogenetic, de-sublimated libidinal model (enlarged times 1000)*. The art in *Sensation* was fatuous, irreligious and sometimes exciting; its radicalism evanescent, reactive, individualistic and resolutely anti-ideological. Like advertising, it demands an immediate response. It has abandoned collective forms of identity and politics and reflects the capitalist logic of the market economy. Like the commodity, it incarnates the instantaneous and the ephemeral. It mirrors our estrangement from ourselves, and is obsessional about the body and sex, but scornful of love and relationships. There is no calling for contemplative appreciation. It stirs up our preconceptions of art, it challenges our settled attitudes about the meaning of culture, but it cannot offer anything of enduring human value. It is art which claws at the possibility of a renaissance in English culture, yet it is unable to imagine and affirm a future.

In the middle of the exhibition, on a white stone base, lay Ron Muick's tiny, perfect replica of his dead father. Despite its trappings of adult maturity – the hair on his legs and abdomen, the lines of age on his face – this father in death is no bigger than the child he had once been. The effigy is more than just a personal memorial, it represents the death of the name and the law of the father. In another gallery Rachel Whiteread's *Ghost*, a large plaster cast of the interior of a room from a Victorian house, conjures up a bygone world of childhood and domesticity. Where there had existed a life of feeling, there is now the solidity of plaster.

In their evocation of loss, both the pieces formed the emotional epicentre of the exhibition. They contradict the audacity and unreflecting brashness of many of the other artists. The tiny effigy and the fossilised adornments of an anonymous room confront us with our own fear of death and nothingness. They give a shape to absence, and they present us with its potential, inviting us to make something of it. It is art as an enactment of farewell. Like Diana's funeral they symbolise the state we are in, a tentative moving beyond ourselves, the search for a new language of politics and ethics.

Tony Blair: An ambivalent approach

In his speech to the 1995 Labour Party conference, Tony Blair made an appeal to the 'lost generation' of 16-24 year-olds by talking about the preoccupations of his own generation.

> Let me talk to you about my generation... We were born into the Welfare State and the NHS, into the market economy of bank accounts, supermarkets, jeans and cars. We had money in our pockets never

dreamt of by our parents ... We built a new popular culture, transformed by colour tv, Coronation Street and the Beatles. We enjoy a
thousand material advantages over any previous generation; and yet we
suffer a depth of insecurity and spiritual doubt they never knew.

Blair represented his generation as 'frightened for our future', living in
'a new age but in an old country'. In a rhetorical flourish he called for
the rebirth of Britain. 'I want us to be a young country again. Young.'
Blair however is ambivalent about youthfulness, with its connotations
of inexperience, irresponsibility and immaturity. In the months before
the 1997 election he redefined his vision as the need to modernise
Britain. His speech to the Party conference was a clarion call to 'Unite
behind our mission to modernise our country for all our people'. His
peroration echoed the quasi religious tone of his speech: 'On May 1,
1997, fear lost. Hope won. The Giving Age began.' Blair's figurative
rhetoric of faith, love, redemption and duty cultivated a presidential
appeal which distanced him from the machinations of instrumental
politics. On the morning of Diana's death, he shaped the mood of the
country when he described her as the people's princess. His emotive
performance in front of the cameras served to highlight the misan-
thropy and dourness of the ancient regime.

Blair has learnt the power of iconic and symbolic politics. Like
Diana he symbolises the future at the same time as he harbours an
ambivalent relationship to his class background. His anodyne vision of
60s popular culture, his non-ideological pursuit of political ambition,
the traces of his religious moralism, and his public homage to his father,
signal that he is a product of a conservative, bourgeois, non-intellectual
and provincial family. This is his natural constituency. But it is one in
which he is ill at ease; Blair is an outsider and a paradox. His rhetoric
reverberates with the symbolic significance of 'newness'. His own relative youthfulness and his winsome good looks evoke the myth of
Kennedy's Camelot. His courtiers exude an ambition and 'nowness'
that comes with power. And yet despite the trappings of modernity,
Blair remains a curiously old fashioned figure, more at home with the
instrumental and rational language of success, than with pleasure and
desire. Like Diana his rebellion against his class has been primarily a
personal and emotional one.

His awkward engagement with his emotions distances him from his
father's middle England, which prides itself on its emotional restraint.
Blair is a man who finds himself in between sensibilities, neither one

thing nor another. His carefully manufactured eclectic musical taste for *Desert Island Discs*, and his gushing, rather coy pre-1997 election interview in the *Sun* about meeting and marrying Cherie Booth, have shown him at his most nervous, and least convincing. He is a part of the urban middle-class generation which broke with the old polarised class system and nuclear family structure of post war Britain. Men in Blair's generation grew up less convinced of their masculine authority than their fathers were, and have a closer identification with their mothers. This indeterminacy of belonging gives him his radicalism because he has few institutional loyalties and little sense of class solidarity. It impels him toward change, and the casting of Britain as a 'young country'. But it is a source of insecurity and it has encouraged him to cultivate a manly authority and certitude. Equally it has invoked in him a nostalgia for 'home'. His politics draws on the allegory of the pilgrim's progress; it is garnered from a religious morality of service and duty in pursuit of a spiritual resting place. In Sedgefield he found one kind of 'authentic' home. At the Labour Party conference in Brighton in 1995 he spoke of the British as 'Decent People. Good people. Patriotic people ... these are "our people"... It is a new Britain. One Britain: the people united by shared values and shared aims.' This appeal to an homogeneous, like-minded race reflects his own need to belong, while denying conflict and difference by conjuring up the image of an idealised family.

In New Labour, Blair is following the longstanding attempt to secure a centre ground in British politics. To do so requires an appeal to a cause greater than the class differences and unequal life chances which divide people. For Joseph Chamberlain it was protectionism and empire, for Mosley it was fascism, for Enoch Powell it was the spectre of a disappearing white, English race. David Owen and the SDP appealed to common sense. Blair stakes his crusade on modernisation and the populist appeal of national togetherness. But, as with the *Sensation* exhibition, Blair's dream of modernisation is circumscribed by the conditions which have produced it. In the months before the 1997 election, New Labour was held in the thrall of an imaginary middle England fashioned during the Thatcher years. The rhetoric of Tony Blair and Jack Straw, in particular, reproduced the family values and disciplinary politics of the Conservatives. Their moral earnestness concerned itself less with a passion for social justice, and more with their ambition for political power. Inevitable perhaps, but it revealed an authoritarianism at variance with the idealism. In the event the old middle England was consumed by its own rancorous disappointments. May 1st revealed a middle England that was, temporarily at least, future oriented and young in spirit, open to differences of sexuality and race, less class-bound, not hemmed in by fear of foreigners, or proper family arrangements, or selfish concern for itself. Blair succeeded in breaking apart the Thatcher hegemony, but his appeal to the people was founded on his own personal mandate. New Labour as a political party was confined to a supporting role.

The consequence of this is a form of governance which, at the time of writing, is in danger of becoming over centralised – run by Blair and a small coterie of personal advisers through the manipulation of the media. Despite its attempts to manage democracy through focus groups, New Labour in government appears to be lagging behind an emerging liberal hegemony in society. An interesting illustration of the possible disparity between New Labour policy-makers and popular sentiment was revealed in research commissioned by NCH Action for Children.[1] The study, carried out by Opinion Leader Research, asked a sample of parents and children, and a group of 'opinion leaders', to rank a given list of problems facing the family. The opinion leaders followed the example of New Labour and graded poor standards in schools as their top priority. In contrast it was ranked only sixth by parents and ninth by children. Most important to parents was drug and alcohol abuse, and for children, violence in the home. On every other issue, bar school standards, the 'opinion leaders' trailed behind the parents and children, particularly on issues of home violence, bullying, lack of facilities for children and young people, and increased materialism. The children outstripped both parents and 'opinion leaders' in their concern for racial discrimination. While this was only a small survey involving less than two thousand individuals and conducted just after the 1997 general election, it points to the central dilemma of New Labour's technocratic and instrumentalist version of modernisation. Blair's symbolic rhetoric of a 'giving society', with its emphasis on feelings and human concern, has no clear conception of social justice and very little idea of an organisational, hegemonic politics which could realise it.

On the Wednesday following the death of Diana, Blair addressed the TUC in Brighton, where he revealed another, waspish and hectoring, side to his character. As if he was laying down the rules to a recalcitrant adolescent, he urged the unions to modernise themselves, accept the flexible labour market and to 'crusade for competitiveness'. He rejected the rights of unions to take solidarity action in line with the International Labour Organisation conventions. 'You don't want it and I won't let it happen' he said. His prescriptive tone revealed the political limitations of New Labour.[2] In many respects New Labour has become the political technocrat's version of old labourism: paternalism replaced by managerialism; smoke filled back rooms replaced by a cult of work efficiency; and its historic suspicion of social movements and autonomous democratic politics now turned on Labour Party members themselves. While Blair exhorts everybody to trust 'the people', he is more tardy when this abstracted, disorganised mass coalesces into an organisation, or a series of political demands. His rhetoric creates a spectacle of concern, without having to actually identify and side with people who are poor, exploited or disadvantaged. This contradiction between the soft focus rhetoric of feelings and the harsh instrumentalist pursuit of power was exposed in the unnecessary debacle over cuts in single parent allowance.

Despite the contradictions in his politics, Blair has harnessed the iconography of emotion, and a popular distrust of instrumental politics, and created the possibility of a new political imaginary. For the first time since 1963 and the Wilson-led, Labour government, a new social democratic settlement could take hold in England. Yet in the face of unprecedented economic and social inequality, the argument for greater equality and fairness has been silenced almost to death. Writing in the November 1997 issue of *Prospect*, John Gray declared Britain to be 'Europe's first post-social democratic society'. In defence of this statement Gray claims that 'there is no public constituency for seriously redistributive taxation in Britain today. But there is a consensus that public expenditure be targeted at the worst off. The political philosophy which best expresses this consensus is not social democracy. It is liberalism.' Gray is opposed to social democracy because he believes it has been too narrowly focused on the overall pattern of distribution of goods in society, when what matters is the well-being of individuals. This is unfair. Advocates of social democracy, particularly those concerned with the alleviation of poverty, have been guided by an ethical concern for the well-being of individuals. Unlike Gray they have recognised the structural nature of inequality and the necessity of state intervention. Gray dislikes the principle of egalitarianism not only because he believes it is unpopular, but because it fails to recognise that inequalities are 'neither fixed not impermeable'. This is partly true (individuals who may be unemployed one year can be in work and better off the following year); but he exaggerates the degree of social mobility in British society, and it allows him to place an unfounded faith in the meritocracy of a deregulated labour market. By underplaying structural inequalities Gray's argument serves to maintain the hegemony of neo-liberal economics in which New Labour is trapped.

To make individual well-being the motivating principle of a politics does not obviate the need for a more collectivist redistribution of goods and services. Personal happiness, contentment, self worth and self fulfilment are, for the overwhelming majority of people, dependent upon economic security. Like Blair, Gray has separated off emotional well-being from instrumental politics. Such a separation is symptomatic of neo-liberalism, which favours consumers over citizens, and seeks to radically reduce the political discourse of democracy in favour of market relations. A defining characteristic of recent public mobilisations – the funeral of Diana, and the protests against the life imprisonment of nineteen year old Louise Woodward in a US court – has been the preeminence of emotional reaction over reasoned politics and debate. A connection between political discourse and the symbolic realm of emotional appeal needs to be established. The question is whether New Labour can raise a serious challenge to neo-liberal orthodoxy by reinvigorating British democracy and by establishing a new form of social democracy – the third way. If this is a possibility, the question begs another. Where are the social forces and constituencies which can create a new ideological politics? The New Labour MP, Denis MacShane, like other modernisers in his party is acutely aware of the fragile nature of New Labour's hold in the country. 'The problem of generation is now a major source of discomfort as the new political elite in Britain seeks to find its bearings and to awaken political engagement'.[3] MacShane is in search of political cadres who will rescue New Labour from an uncertain future, and wonders where he is going to find them. New Labour needs a soul, and it needs a bolster in order to assert itself in favour of EMU, challenge the vested interests of the City, and break its subservience to Murdoch's press. MacShane sets his sights on a new generation. As for his own generation, he dismisses it as 'the most useless, self-indulgent, whinging, narcissistic bunch of good-for-nothings in world history'. He places his faith in the young.

New Labour's search for a young Britain continues the long romance of British radicalism with youth. But in the 1990s the myth of a golden age of youth has become tarnished. This is not simply due to the hard times of young people, or any greater sobriety on their part.

The jaundiced outlook belongs to those of Blair's and MacShane's generation who were formed by the political and cultural ideals of '1968'. A sense of political defeat has given many a more pessimistic outlook on the possibilities for social change, and the political and cultural potential of today's young. For some, the young are the products of neo-liberal economics and consumer culture: apolitical, their attention spans limited to three minutes, pursuing individual ambition to the detriment of social solidarity. For those radicalised in the late 1960s and early 1970s, the late 1980s marked the advent of a significant political and cultural gap between generations. The new forms of politics developed in the earlier generation lost their appeal. Young people are not using the same political languages as their parents. Major innovations in music (techno, drum and bass) and computer technologies, the pervasiveness of the media in the lives of young people, the emergence of social purity movements around animal rights and environmentalism, plus a general 'feel bad factor' about Politics (with a capital P) have contributed to this generation gap. The young have moved camp; they've gone somewhere else currently off the political perceptual map of the older generation. It's not just New Labour that's in trouble – the generation of 1968 have also lost the *Weltanschauung*.

The abandonment of the market

Last summer, I was waiting for a bus at King's Cross in London. The tube had broken down and there was a fractious air of impatience amongst the people waiting for the inevitably late bus. In the midst of the growing crowd, the bus shelter was empty. I looked inside. A young boy was lying fast asleep on a piece of cardboard, covered by an old grey blanket. His finger nails were rimmed with dirt, his hands filthy. He'd taken off his trainers and they were neatly placed beside his head. He was about fifteen to seventeen years old and oblivious to the crowd which massed around him. Nobody entered the shelter. People knew he was there, but had tacitly established a perimeter fence, a cordon sanitaire between themselves and the boy. An older man, drunk and semi-stupified, stopped as if he was going to enter and break the invisible boundary. As he swayed across the threshold it seemed tantamount to a physical assault and I realised that the crowd's refusal to make any claim on the bus shelter was not simply a fear of being assaulted or contaminated, but a way of protecting the boy and granting him a little dignity. The old man just looked and then walked off. The squalid, litter strewn space remained still and quiet; a teenager's surrogate bedroom at the bottom of the heap.

In 1988 Nicholas Scott, then minister for social security, withdrew benefits for 16 and 17 year olds. He took his cue from tabloid stories of unemployed youth living it up in an endless round of South Coast boarding houses: 'It is not the government's job to give an incentive to people to leave home'. By 1996 his peevish action had succeeded in making destitute thousands of young people. The Children's Society estimated that 50,000 young people, most aged about fifteen, the majority escaping abuse, ran away from home each year. The same year Shelter reported a disturbingly high proportion of 16 and 17 year olds amongst the homeless callers to its emergency night line. During the summer, Barnardos reported that 8000 young people leaving local authority care were threatened with this netherworld. Seventy-five per cent had no academic qualifications. Between 50 per cent and 80 per cent were jobless. One in seven of the young women were pregnant or already mothers. Thirty per cent of them will end up homeless.[4] The 1990s witnessed the deepening and extension of the deregulated market, the decline of welfare and the growth of the anti-democratic state. This small minority of young homeless bear the remorseless logic of these developments: deserted by the state, family destroyed, without qualifications, without cultural capital, their labour no longer a commodity of any value; there is little left but the intertwined economies of prostitution, drugs and crime. By 1997 the life stories of these young people were coming to light. The little reported North Wales Tribunal, under Sir Ronald Waterhouse QC, was cataloguing the systematic rape and abuse of young boys and girls in local authority children's homes. Unscrupulous men, upright members of the middle-classes, public figures and care workers pillaged children's homes for their own sexual gratification. And as a cold spell bit in late October, the charity Centreprise reported inquiries from the young homeless were up 14 per cent on the previous year.

In 1995 Centaur Marketing ran their annual conference 'Targeting The Youth Market' at the Cafe Royal in London. The central question before the assembled delegates was: 'Can the youth market be success-fully targeted by socio-economic background?' The long and the short of it was that it could not. In his presentation, John Grant, planning director of St Luke's advertising agency, argued that a singular youth culture which could be defined by its socio-economic location no longer existed. The 16-24 year old group was very difficult to divide into coherent categories. There was diversity, there was difference, there were markets within markets, there was a fluidity of identities which were in the continuous process of being redefined. He argued that it was much easier to describe the ingredients of their culture than to describe *them*. He quoted the Henley Centre: one third of all 15-24 year olds claim to have been to a rave. Rave culture has touched the lives of more under-25s than all previous youth cultures put together. But try to categorise 'rave' and it fragments into a variety of sub-texts. Forget the style tribes, forget categories, said Grant . . . use signifiers, use culture; target the young through their varying, virtual connections to the media; grab them as *Loaded* readers, fans of *Friends* or the *X Files*. Consumerism has played a pivotal role in creating youth cultural identities. But today's generation of 16-24 year olds are a tricky commercial proposition. The global marketplace has transformed youth cultures and their signs of revolt and rebellion into commodities and an aesthetic of 'youth'. Youth cultural commodities are no longer confined to young people. Advertisers are in the business of freezing the calvacade of street aspirations, pleasures and identities into instantly recognisable sound-bites and images, long enough to commodify an aspirational identity and attach it to a product. But attempting to define 'youth' has become a perennial problem as youth cultures fragment, metamorphose or become parodies of themselves.

Young people are also an unknown quantity to psephologists, political pundits and career politicians: in the 1992 general election 2.5 million of the 18-25 age group did not vote. Nearly one in five young people did not even appear on the electoral register. New Labour, recognising its own profound cultural and political estrangement from young people, set out to win over first time voters for the 1997 election. The 'lost generation' was invented. Gordon Brown announced a new windfall tax on the profits of the public utilities which would finance the creation of youth training and employment. New Labour offered the young a contract of rights and responsibilities. The Ministry of Sound launched its own advertising campaign to encourage youth registration and voting. A Rock the Vote musical tour embarked on the same quest. In one respect it was successful: Mark Leonard and Sundera Katwala claim that it was the swing of 19 per cent amongst 18-29 year olds which helped to explain New Labour's landslide win.[5] But the impact on the longer term trend in youthful indifference to electoral politics was negligible. The 1992 level of only 43 per cent of 18-

24 year olds voting remained almost unaffected. As Mike Kenny argues in this book, the problem of young people's apathy towards parliamentary democracy runs deep, and to overcome it requires changes in the culture and political structures of our society.

In the last twenty years British capitalism has undergone a modernisation which has transformed its economic structure and its class culture and consciousness. Amongst the young, traditional work-based solidarities which once defined personal identity have been superseded by identities defined by consumption, lifestyle and leisure activities. The deregulation of the labour market – the growth of temporary jobs, flexibility of working hours, decentralisation of the work site and short-term contracts – the decline of full-time male employment and the expansion of part-time female work have contributed to an individualisation of society. Traditional forms of class and gender consciousness have been disrupted as people have been freed from traditional class and gender role prescriptions. Individualisation has not ended class as an organising category of capitalism, rather it has fragmented class cultural consciousness and consequently undermined the old forms of political mobilisation. There now exists a new sense of personal autonomy and individual choice, but one which is curtailed by the sharp increase in economic inequality and by new forms of institutional regulation. In 1979 6 per cent of households had neither adult partner working; in 1997 the figure is just under 20 per cent. The 1996 Rowntree Foundation's *Inquiry into Income and Wealth* reported that the numbers living on less than half of average incomes had trebled since 1978. The richest 10 per cent of the population now controls the same amount of income as the poorer half of the population: approximately one quarter of total income. For the poorest 10 per cent incomes are no higher than they were two decades ago. The cause of this all-pervasive growth in the gap between the rich and the poor are the inequalities structured into the labour market and the decline in value of social security and pensions.[6] The summary impact of inequality has been disproportionately felt by the young. Sixty per cent of 15-24 year olds have a disposable income of less than £50 per week.[7]

Gender, education and work

In 1996 16-25 year olds constituted 13.3 per cent of the population. They made up 17 per cent of the workforce (compared to 23 per cent in 1986) and 35 per cent of the long-term unemployed. Despite the freezing of student grants, and a growing reluctance amongst the young to be saddled with the burden of debt, almost one third now enter higher education compared to 1 in 7 in 1987. Between April 1993 and April 1997 there was a fall in unemployment amongst under 25s from 17.3 per cent to 13.6 per cent. With the announcement of Gordon Brown's New Deal and the government's pledge to take 250,000 young people aged 18-24 off benefit and into work, unemployment in this target group declined, but as Ian Brinkley argues in his chapter 'Underworked and Underpaid', the circumstances of young people, relative to the rest of the workforce, have worsened. The neo-liberal economic orthodoxy, that people should follow the logic of the market and price themselves into jobs, has proved false. Between April 1984 and April 1996 hourly earnings for young men fell from 82.8 per cent of average to 72.8 per cent, while young women's hourly earnings fell from 70.5 per cent of the average to 65.8 per cent. A survey carried out in 1994 by the Labour Research Department (commissioned by the GMB) reported that 30 per cent of jobs offered to young people yielded a net income below the income support threshold; fifty per cent offered between £3 and £4 per hour. The situation for young black British and British Asians is more difficult. As Balbir Chatrik describes, the majority of young black unemployed are concentrated in 18 of Britain's 471 local authority areas. In the London Borough of Kensington and Chelsea, for example, unemployment amongst the black group is 70 per cent, compared to 6 per cent for the comparable white group. Young blacks and Asians are more likely than their white peers to be employed in jobs which have poor terms and conditions. *The Social Focus on Ethnic Minorities* (HMSO), published in 1996, showed sharp disparities in the ethnic distribution of income. Amongst Pakistani and Bangladeshi people the average full-time, hourly rate of pay was £4.78 for women and £6.87 for men, compared with £6.59 for white women and £8.34 for white men.

For the majority of those young people who have had the least opportunities in education, employment prospects are confined to the non-unionised sectors of catering, retailing and services. Here they experience an unrestrained version of the new managerial ethos in which the worker shoulders the risks and insecurities of the company's market performance. Without education and the acquisition of cultural capital – and even this provides no guarantees – the future offers only the insecurities of unemployment or working poverty. Thus Balbir

Chatrik welcomes the New Deal in that it recognises that the training and educational 'gateways' into the labour market are a crucial factor in determining individual life chances. Karen Triggs's essay on the Welfare to Work pilot project analyses the impact of the New Deal on the lives of young single mothers. This transitional period of young people's lives – the move from education into work – has become the site of new forms of class struggle as the social classes compete for best entry positions into the employment market. This struggle is inflected by race and gender relations.

Statistics released by the Department of Education in 1995 suggested that white, working-class boys were at the bottom of the educational system. Figures showed that 37 per cent of boys were achieving five or more A-C GCSE grades compared to 45.9 per cent of girls. Chris Woodhead, the Chief Inspector of Schools, wrote in *The Times* on 6 March 1996: 'The failure of boys, and in particular white working-class boys, is one of the most disturbing problems we face within the whole education system'. This trend was confirmed in January 1998 by new figures on GCSE results which revealed the gap in achievement between girls and boys had increased considerably. In contrast to the educational disenfranchisement of white, particularly working-class boys, 50 per cent of young black eighteen year olds were still in full-time education, compared with 30 per cent of whites. However the rise of school exclusions in England – from 3,000 in 1990 to over 11,000 in 1993 were made up of a disproportionate number of black boys, presaging the very high rates of unemployment amongst young black men (see the Runnymede Trust's *True Stories and Pressures in Brixton*, 1996). The OFSTED inspections of 1993-1994 revealed the exclusion rate amongst black Caribbean pupils was almost six times higher than the rate amongst white pupils. Despite the problems facing young black men, young people from ethnic minorities are now over-represented in higher education. Young black and Asian women are doing the best of all, suggesting that they are using education as a strategy for gaining social inclusion.[8] As yet these higher rates of achievement in education have not been reflected in patterns of work and pay.

There are plenty who believe that the superior educational attainments of girls signals a more egalitarian culture and the redundancy of feminist battles for equality. However the panic which began in the mid-1990s over the under-performance of boys has diverted attention away from the continuing, traditional inequalities of gender. Research carried out by Barclays Bank published in 1997 uncovered a striking disparity in the starting salaries of male and female graduates.[9] Men started work on a typical salary of £13,660, compared to women's starting salary of £11,749 – a difference of 16 per cent – double what it was in 1995. In addition, the research revealed that women's educational performance was not being translated into their winning the better jobs. Women also had low expectations of their future earning power, a pessimism which proved to be well founded when the Equal Opportunities Commission announced that the gender pay gap on hourly wages had narrowed by just 7 per cent in twenty years. In 1996 men averaged £9.39 per hour, compared to £7.50 for women. The educational achievements of girls, and the time and energy invested in their education, too often ends in discrimination, disappointment and frustration in the labour market.

Individualisation has freed today's young women from the old gendered expectations of motherhood and homemaking. Their own mothers grew up in domestic cultures which ascribed, as part of the natural order, gendered roles and behaviours. At the heart of post-war consumer capitalism, and its transmogrification of social and economic relations, the middle-class family was a world where nature still appeared to determine one's destiny. By the 1960s the market had begun to undermine the structures of the nuclear family. New ideologies of individual choice cut across women's until then accepted position as wives and mothers, and excarcebated the growing tension between the structures of gender inequality and the growing consciousness of female autonomy. By the end of the 1960s the gendered relations of many, particularly middle-class, families were beset by an intense ambivalence over the role of women and the nature of femininity. In contrast, the invasion of modernity into the family had reinforced men's traditional role. The sexual revolution encouraged the expansion of male heterosexual autonomy and personal status without any accompanying change in the structures of gender inequality: the domestic division of labour remained intact, men continued to monopolise full-time wage labour, and the market and institutions privileged them over women. But women's growing consciousness, that choice rather than fate could determine their lives, challenged the ideologies of male authority. Masculine roles and behaviours were increasingly brought into question. The decline of female 'gender fate' enabled girls to acquire a greater degree of independence from the prescribed roles of their mothers; but, conversely, it had the effect of reinforcing boys' identification with their mothers.

Despite a loosening identification with traditional male roles, men were still relatively free of social and economic contradictions until the onset of unemployment and de-industrialisation in the 1980s. Even then men remained relatively uninterested in the predicaments of their gender identities. Men experienced the central conflicts of modernisation through women. Women prompted change in the private realm of parenting, sexuality, emotions and psychological wellbeing, precipitating personal crises for men and a recognition of their emotional dependency on women. For the grandchildren of the 1960s, this changing dynamic of gender relations has influenced their own response to the new uncertainties of the 1990s. Young women appear to have a greater social confidence. Part of the legacy of feminism has been a transformation in young women's attitudes and aspirations. In contrast to young women's ambition to succeed, however, many young men appear to be floundering (although, as a whole group, they still maintain their gendered privilege). Individualisation, coupled with the rise in male redundancy and the increasing numbers of women in employment, has undermined the old rules and roles – so much so that they can no longer assume an allotted place in society. The scorn amongst many young working-class men for work which uses educational and mental skills suggests that they have failed to recognise the technological revolution which is transforming the nature of men's work. But their self-deception is partly due to their fear of failing to match the social confidence, interpersonal skills and intellectual dexterity of young women. Divested of hope and a productive role in society, unable to achieve adult independence, and unwilling to contribute to the domestic economy of their mothers' homes, many young men in the 1990s simply gave up.

Male redundancy created cultures of prolonged adolescence in which young male identities remain locked into the locality of estate, shops and school. Violence, criminality, drug-taking and alcohol consumption become the means to gaining prestige for a masculine identity bereft of any social value or function. A Home Office report, *Young People and Crime* (1996), based on 2,500 interviews, confirmed this prolongation of young men's anti-social adolescent behaviour. One half of the teenage boys and one third of the girls interviewed had been involved in criminal activity. By their mid twenties young women have grown out of crime, only 4 per cent admitting to anything more serious than taking drugs. In contrast, the figure for men of a similar age was 31 per cent. Men were less likely to have left home, less likely to be in stable relationships and less likely to have secure employment. The researchers found only a weak link between crime and social class. The pattern of prolonged adolescence extended beyond areas of economic deprivation. Ineptitude in interpersonal skills, which so often passes for appropriate masculine behaviour, leaves young men ill-equipped to cope with social isolation and despair. In Britain in 1982, according to the Office of Population Censuses and Statistics, 320 young men aged between 15 and 24 killed themselves. In 1992 the number was 500, an increase of 56 per cent. Young women too are under duress. Evidence of depression is twice as high amongst women while their incidence of 'suicidal behaviour' (as opposed to actual suicide) is also higher. Michael Rutter and David J. Smith in their report, *Psychosocial Disorders in Young People* (1996) deny that this increase in mental ill-health is a consequence of social and economic deprivation; they argue that it is a result of the changing nature of adolescence and young people's isolation from the rest of society. It is perhaps young men who are most detached, socially and emotionally, from family life, encouraging a trend which will see men under pensionable age as the largest category of single householders by the year 2011 (*Social Trends* 1996).

Parental control

These vicissitudes, combined with the withdrawal of state support from young people, have made access to family support crucial. Youth unemployment and the increase in post-compulsory education have extended the period of young people's dependency on their parents (64 per cent of 16-24 year olds live with their parents). The Conservative government encouraged this trend and sought to institutionalise it in legislation. The Job Seeker's Allowance, introduced in October 1996, is designed to keep unemployed people under twenty-four at home with their parents and confirmed the state's attempt to use the family as an institution of labour discipline and social order. Young people have suffered the most severe cuts to their benefit. Single 18-24 year olds lost £10 per week (a loss of £540 per year) under the new scheme, forcing them to rely on their families for financial support and creating intolerable stresses amongst the poor and badly paid. The JSA intensifies pressure on the unemployed to take low paid work. By requiring them to develop a personal employability plan, it shifts the responsibility for unemployment onto the moral and personal conduct of the individual. In the context of pluralised underemployment and a 'disorganised' labour market, the effect is to blur the boundary between being in work and being out of work. Unemployment as a linguistic concept ceases to exist. The effect is to drive thousands of young people off benefit and out of the mainstream economy altogether, either into an indefinite dependency on their families or into illicit forms of money making.

Enforced economic dependency takes away young people's cultural, social and personal autonomy and denies them any semblance of citizenship. It is this antagonism between the cultural expectations of the young, and the inability of the economic system to realise them, that has been the major source of youth unrest and the principal site of the state's political intervention in young people's lives. Since the 1980s, New Right social reformers, intellectuals and politicians have challenged the social presumption of young people's rights to self determination. Their ambition was to regenerate the discursive machinery which has defined and regulated 'the adolescent' and 'youth' (criminal justice system, civil and family law, schooling, employment and social security legislation). In 1986 David Marsland, in a melodramatically entitled essay, 'Young People Betrayed' (written for the right-wing think-tank, The Social Affairs Unit) called for the restoration of the family's responsibility for young people.[10] He argued that society should stop treating young people as if they were adults and recognise their need for caring support and firm leadership. His first concern was the increasing divorce rate which had to be slowed down through changes in social attitudes and in the legal and procedural frameworks which he believed made divorce 'far too common and far too easy'. Next, he argued that the monopoly of the liberal educational establishment over young people's lives should be removed by handing responsibility for education back to parents. The grants system in further and higher education, which enabled young people to pursue 'inappropriate studies' and led to their 'bewitchment . . . by the pied pipers of campus peer groups', should also be abolished. Parents, aided by a system of loans, could retain control over their student offspring by being responsible for financing them through college. Finally Marsland proposed the removal of all rights to benefit for the unemployed young. By 1997 his cranky aspirations for the regulation of young people were either already in effect or had moved to the centre of political debate.

During the middle years of the 1990s, the governing classes of both major political parties adopted a moralising rhetoric about the young. The emphasis on the personal regulation of moral conduct was evident in the rise of Tony Blair and the technocratic transformation of the Labour Party as it accommodated the deregulated market economy. New Labour, seeking to locate the unmanageable macro-problems of social dislocation in what they believed to be the manageable personal behaviours of individuals, adopted Amitai Etzioni and his idea of communitarianism. Etzioni offered a link between liberalism and the new politics of social discipline by making the Victorian, imperial language of character-building respectable again: 'Character formation lays the psychic foundation for the ability both to mobilise to a task and to behave morally by being able to control impulses and defer gratification'.[11] New Labour's early policy approach to the young had much in common with the old Victorian improving organisations like the Boys' Brigade, which disseminated the ideals and practices of the public schools' religion of character-building in an attempt to bring social discipline to the working classes. Peter Mandelson and Roger Liddle, promoting their book *The Blair Revolution – Can New Labour Deliver?* in *The Guardian* (27 February, 1996) were succinct in their no-nonsense carrot and stick approach:

> Britain urgently needs to put in place a new contract between society and young people . . . to help young people find a sure footing in the adult world, but with tough penalties for those who refuse the opportunity and fail to fulfil their side of the bargain.

In defence of its politics of social discipline, New Labour cited the language of citizens' rights and responsibilities. But their version of citizenship did not guarantee social and economic equality, and without a determined effort to tackle the injustices of inequality, it was a rhetoric which betrayed an authoritarian, bullying streak, with the easier targets of the poor and powerless coming in for the most moral condemnation.

Young Britain: time for dialogue

Blair's pitch for youthful support has revealed his uncertainty about whether to take a detached and paternal approach, or to risk a more open identification. Blair is going to be remembered by many young people for his authoritarian pronouncement on homework, his rigid and puritanical attitude toward soft drugs, and an insistent representation of young people as a cause of social disorder. His moral earnestness has favoured a prescriptive tone of voice, rather than an encouraging one. Not surprising then, that the early enthusiasm of pop stars for 'Cool Britannia' has waned. Despite this, he remains an attractive, if ambiguous, figure to young people. New Labour needs to win the active support of young people by creating a dialogue rather than through the presumption of imposing policy initiatives. If they choose to listen, they'll find a generation where there are sophisticated opinions and untapped ideals. As Elaine Pennicott argues in her piece about the new black British popular fiction, young black Britons, despite their exclusion from the mainstream, are engaged in important and creative ways with the cultural life of this country. Similarly, Bilkis Malek's essay on young British Asians suggests no hint of cultural or political inertia on their part. But here are two social groups whose cultural and social visibility is still confined to stereotypical images. Despite their over-representation in higher education, their reservoir of talent, ambition and determination is still largely ignored.

Noshin Ahmad, in her support for the hijab (or veil), is a challenge to Britain's post-colonial culture. The attempt amongst young, British, Muslim women to fashion an Islamic response to white, British culture is creating new meanings of being both Muslim and British. In recent years the veil has presented white feminists and liberals with a dilemma. Enlightenment secularism is antipathetic toward religious and moral dictates which have sought to order and codify the body. Liberal, European feminism has been a struggle by women to secure their bodies for themselves, against religion and against the male gaze, and to do this through the notion of self-expression and individuality. The veil appears to contradict this historical struggle, and it is consequently often viewed by European liberals as archaic, reactionary and detrimental to the status and position of women. Ahmad and other educated young, Muslim women argue for a presentation of femininity that stands in sharp contrast to the long (Eurocentric) history of white European women's struggle for self-determination. The veil touches on a central incommensurability between two traditions and cultures. And as Bilkis Malek points out in her essay, it is one further example of the limitations of current post-colonial theorising of racial difference, and the liberal notion of cultural hybridity.

Peter Gartside's incisive look at the politics of eco-protests reveals an imaginative and innovative movement which has become deeply politicised by the Criminal Justice Act. This is a generation which shares a common apathy toward Westminster's brand of politics. As Mike Kenny describes in 'That's Entertainment', the need to establish connections between young people and the political community is an apparently intractable problem for modern states. Youth cultures are fashioned out of the market and popular culture, not through the civic discourses of democratic politics, and they find no representation in the preoccupations and language of a culturally homogeneous, self-referential party politics. Young people today lack defined political identifications with which to communicate collective hopes and griev-ances. This absence of institutionalised forms of representation, combined with the social exclusion and impoverishment of large sections of young people, is creating a crisis of democracy. Peter Gartside's concluding comment on the need to engage *politically* with modernity, raises once again the popular anti-rationalism which has been a reaction to the managerial and instrumental nature of reasoned, democratic politics.

Where the media has represented an identifiable politics within the 16-24 generation – DIY and eco-protest – its character has been funda-mentally antagonistic to the culture and ethos of New Labour. In contrast to New Labour's image of a party of capitalist modernisation, these politics have often turned to anti-modern, anti-rationalist values. Young people have been at the forefront of counter-cultures, searching for the re-enchantment of contemporary life in the mediaeval commu-nities of travellers, animal rights, the mysticism of paganism and tree-huggers and the holistic rhetoric of rave culture. As Gartside argues, it is a politics which is simultaneously here and not here; ephemeral, tran-sient, disorganised. Divining the attitudes and values of this generation has meant looking to their cultural, artistic and musical expression. As Rupa Huq shows in 'Paradigm Lost?' it is here that the nascent languages and sensibilities of the new generation have been given shape.

New Labour in power must win a cultural hegemony which will help it to achieve a second term in office. The energy, innovation and idealism of young people are central to achieving this task. Not only can a new generation help to secure the new cultural, gendered and ethnic meanings of middle England, its political commitment is essential if New Labour wants to realise its ambition to be a great reforming government. New Labour has to foster ideological connections between the cultures and activities of young people and a democratising state. Instead of trying to co-opt young people into its own political machinery it has to develop a dialogue with them. It means listening to and learning from the sounds and images coming from youth cultures, ending the prescriptive, hectoring tone inherited from communitarianism, and developing a politics which encourages the aspirations of young people. Jonathan Keane's essay on Ecstasy puts forward a persuasive image of a generation that is both idealistic and disenchanted; one which has created a drug culture that has become 'an ode to lost joy'. The fear and silence amongst politicians around the issue of drugs serves only to increase youthful cynicism with politicians and adults in general. When their own children are found to be a part of the drug culture they so consistently condemn, the resulting farce – as in the case of Jack Straw's son – is laughable. We need a return to idealism, and that requires risk-taking and innovation on the part of political leaders. The TUC's New Unionism is about developing a political culture of organising which will depend on the collective idealism of young people for its success. Frances O'Grady writes about an initiative which is rooted in the experiences of the early civil rights workers in the deep South of the United States, the American peace corps, and our own Community Service Volunteers. If Denis MacShane is to find New Labour's soul, the government will need to respond positively to these kinds of initiatives. A powerful gesture to begin with would be the introduction of a decent minimum wage, which includes young people. It would send a clear and bold message that politics can make a real difference to their lives. They might then listen. A conversation might begin.

There is something intangible about discussing a new generation. In one sense it only begins to exist when it is invented in books like this. We can pin to it our hopes, fantasies and anxieties, compare it to its predecessors, lament its lack of collective political inspiration, be impressed by its plurality and its social liberalism. In the end what is important is to encourage dialogue across the generations and to create an opportunity to explore the nature of generational differences, similarities and connections. I hope this book is a part of a growing response to the political and economic predicaments of young people. There have been significant changes and differences between the radical politics generated in the 1970s (class, anti-racism, feminism, gay liberation) and the radical politics of the 1990s. But as George McKay has shown in his book *Senseless Acts of Beauty* continuity has existed in the politics and practices of the counterculture, dating back to the free hippy festivals of the 1960s, on through punk subcultures to present day eco-radicals and young people's resistance to the Criminal Justice Act. Equally, and more important, there remains a continuity in what I can only call the ordinariness of people's lives; the aspirations for love, a good life, useful, properly paid employment, pleasure and happiness. Young people today are faced with a qualitatively different society from the one their parents grew up in. Their political economy reveals a great deal about the ongoing restructuring of British capitalism and its class system, just as their cultures of resistance reflect the current strengths and weaknesses of radical democratic politics.

Notes

1. See *Family Life: The Age of Anxiety*, NCH Action for Children Publications, 1997.
2. For an interesting discussion on the relationship between Blair's symbolic politics of affect and the instrumental, rational business of politics, see Wendy Wheeler's essay on mourning and modernity in Mark Perryman, ed., *The Moderniser's Dilemma*, Lawrence & Wishart, 1998.
3. Denis MacShane, 'Tomorrow's values may be more radical than we think', in *Critical Quarterly*, Volume 39, No.3, Autumn 1997.
4. See *Too Much Too Young – The Failure of Social Policy in Meeting the Needs of Care Leavers*, Barnado's, 1996.
5. Mark Leonard and Sunder Katwala, 'Youth and Politics', in *Renewal*, Vol.5, nos 3&4, 1997.
6. Alissa Goodman, Paul Johnson and Steven Webb, *Inequality in the UK*, Oxford University Press, 1997.
7. See *Never had it so good? The truth about being young in 90s Britain*, The British Youth Council, Barnado's, 1996.
8. See Heidi Safia Mirza's argument about young black women's strategies to succeed at school, in *Education Today and Tomorrow*, Vol 49, No.1, Spring 1997 and in Heidi Safia Mirza, *Black British Feminism*, Routledge, 1997.
9. See the Money section of *The Guardian*, Saturday, 5 April, 1997.
10. David Marsland, 'Young People Betrayed', in Digby Anderson, ed., *Full*

Circle? Bringing up Children in the Post-Permissive Society, Social Affairs Unit, 1988.
11. Amitai Etzioni, 'Learning Right from Wrong', in *Demos Quarterly*, Issue 1, Winter, 1993.

The us generation

Frances O'Grady

One warm Saturday night in July 1997, restaurant goers in London's fashionable Covent Garden piazza were confronted by an unusual spectacle. A determined band of young people were shinning up lamp-posts to unfurl flags and calling on workers to join a union. The young trade unionists, led by organiser Louise Chinnery, had designated Covent Garden a *respect at work zone* and the event marked the start of a concerted organising drive among the locality's army of mainly young, low-paid workers.

Louise is just one of a new generation of organisers breathing fresh life into the union movement. Over the past year, she has signed up hundreds of workers in shops and factories across the notoriously hard to organise South East region and, this summer, is leading a new recruitment campaign targeting bars, clubs and restaurants in the heart of London's West End.

Many of the revellers in Covent Garden that night were disturbed to discover that those serving their top price meals were paid as little as £3 an hour. 'Outing' low-paying bosses, raising customer awareness and winning public support is a hallmark of the new style trade unionism which aims to kickstart membership back into growth. The organising campaign aims to go beyond recruitment to building an active membership whereby young people feel connected, involved and empowered through collective organisation.

For Louise Chinnery, organising workers brings its own rewards: 'We came out of the workplace, and I just thought, "YES!" What a feeling – there's nothing else like it. We've helped people to change their lives, to look after themselves at work. There's no other job I know of where you get that kind of feeling.'

But the newly emerging 'youth wing' of the union movement may present as big a challenge to prevailing union culture as to the businesses it aims to organise. Unions are waking up to the need to recruit young people, but are they ready for the consequences of young people's involvement? As one of the new crop of organisers commented: 'People get their own power bases and are very reluctant to let go and pass it on to the next generation. They may not agree with the direction we take but they need to respect that'.

Unions may have no choice. Membership was hit hard by years of Tory union-bashing. While in recent years the rate of loss has slowed, TUC membership has declined dramatically from around half the workforce before the Conservatives took power in 1979, to just under 7 million today. The crisis of falling union membership and rising inequality are one and the same. In the first five years of Tory rule alone, the poorest suffered a cut in real income while the richest were awarded a massive 60 per cent hike in pay.

The contrast between union Britain and non-union Britain is stark. Union members get better pay, holidays and training than their non-union counterparts. There is a growing body of evidence that unionisation adds value not only to employees, but to the firm and the economy too. The vast majority of Britain's most successful businesses already recognise unions. But while the reins of power have changed hands at Westminster, too many boardrooms are still controlled by those for whom trade unions remain *the enemy within*.

Young people are at the sharp end of non-unionism. One in three take home less than £100 a week, three quarters have no right to protection against the sack, and according to the TUC *Testament of Youth* survey, half of young workers say they are treated unfairly at work.

Young workers, more than anyone, have most to gain from sticking together and joining a union. Yet in Britain today, only one in five under 25 year-olds holds a union card and teenage membership hangs by a thread. The problem isn't that young workers no longer need unions, the problem is that unions have failed to reach them. For the best part of two decades, young workers have been crowded into low pay, high turnover Mcjobs where unions are weak. Too many have never even heard of unions – let alone been asked to join one.

Union organisers face a further obstacle. Young people may have high hopes for the future but expectations of the here and now are distressingly low. According to the TUC's newly appointed youth officer Mark Holding: 'They don't have a benchmark of what's a good place to work. There are extremely low expectations. They feel they're no worse off than their friends so it follows that the boss must be an OK bloke'.

The TUC's New Unionism campaign has a twin-track strategy of building existing membership bases and breaking new ground. With nearly 4 million non-union workers employed in workplaces covered by recognition agreements, there is plenty of scope to 'mop up'. But in the longer term, unions need to build new bases where jobs are growing and where young people are more likely to be found. The Labour government's promise of new rights – including the right to union recognition – should help soften the ground for organising. But as communities across Britain know all too well, individual rights count for little without strong organisation to back them up.

Throughout history, young people have always been on the frontline of social change. Unions are now making a special appeal for their help to rebuild the movement and win workplace justice. In the autumn of 1997 the University of North London hosted *interActiv* – the first ever national event organised jointly by the National Union of Students and the TUC New Unionism campaign. *interActiv*, which offered a mix of debates and skills-based events, aimed to attract young workers to trade unionism, including students who increasingly must earn in order to learn.

interActiv set out to challenge what is described as the 'myth' of the me generation. The rejection of the notion that young people today are intrinsically apathetic and individualistic chimes a chord with another young organiser Dawn Butler: 'I'm sick of people saying that young people are just not interested. I remember sitting at the back of a union meeting when someone said that and I'm thinking, but I'm a young person and I'm interested.'

Feedback from the *interActiv* knowledge zone confirmed that ignorance rather than apathy is the key obstacle. 'So, what *is* a union exactly?' was the most common enquiry received by trade unionists staffing the information point, providing a poignant reminder of the scale of the education task which lies ahead. According to union officials, young people had a voracious appetite for information and with a throughput of well over 200 young people, activity in the knowledge zone exceeded expectations.

interActiv was experimental in its form as well as content. The informal 'turn up on the day' approach ensured that the organisation of the various zones sometimes veered between creativity and chaos. One workshop, which offered an eclectic mix of discussion spanning sport, culture and corporate campaigning, culminated in a heated debate on the plight of the Liverpool dockers. While in other speak-outs young workers grappled with the need to campaign for a genuinely national minimum wage, students tended to be more preoccupied with the imminent impact of tuition fees. A workshop on organising skills provided the promising common ground for young trade unionists and single issue campaigners alike. Consequently, future *interActiv* events plan to focus more sharply on talent scouting young people for a development programme in leadership and organising skills through a series of targeted, locally based training events. The next stage of *interActiv* may be less ambitious in its scale and public profile, but may well prove to be more productive in meeting the target of developing a new corps of young union leaders.

Such events will help develop a pool of potential trainee lead organisers for the TUC's new Organising Academy. A modest advertising campaign for 25 trainee organisers generated 4,000 responses in one month alone. The academy, which opened its doors in January 1998, aims to give young people from a rich variety of backgrounds the chance to help workers to stand up for their rights. It offers a twelve-month quality training programme, some of it in the classroom, but most of it on the job. Trainees are sponsored by individual unions but all get the same decent wage and conditions. Previous union experience helps but isn't essential. Involvement in anti-racist, environmental, women's, lesbian and gay and other community campaigns counts too. And all trainees must have the commitment, talent and enough gritty determination to win through.

New Unionism draws its inspiration in part from the rejuvenation of its sister union centre in the United States, the AFL-CIO. After years of membership loss, AFL-CIO has just announced a rise in membership – the first for 30 years. Membership growth in the USA has been won on the back of a massive shift of resources, and people, away from servicing a dwindling base of traditional union strongholds towards organising workers in the new services and industries. Its new leader, John Sweeney, explicitly rejects business unionism in favour of social activism. The AFL-CIO's Organising Institute is training hundreds of organisers concentrating mainly on 'greenfield' sites and the strategy is underpinned by building alliances with other progressive social movements with a strong youth focus.

Sweeney is also the brain behind some of the innovative campaign techniques being used to expose corporate greed, anti-unionism and unfair treatment. Following hard on the heels of last year's Union Summer initiative whereby over one thousand campus student volunteers were deployed to help organise America's low wage Sunbelt, the AFL-CIO launched a Union Cities campaign. Union Cities is pushing for 'economic development strategies that create jobs and growth while establishing worker and family-friendly community standards for local industries and public investment', and its *street heat* initiative specifically targets hostile employers who refuse union recognition. Street heat has already notched up successes, winning public support from local politicians and community leaders, and mobilising youthful *rapid response teams* in solidarity with union organising drives.

The North American experience of experimenting with new techniques to beat hostile employers and win union recognition holds important lessons for a British union movement looking to organise young workers. The biggest barrier to membership identified by young manual workers and those in the private sector, in a survey by the public service union UNISON, was 'my boss won't let me'.

Support for the organising model is gaining ground in the British trade union movement. Research by Jeremy Waddington of Warwick University's Industrial Relations and Research Unit shows that the overwhelming reason why people join unions is not discount shopping deals and cheap credit cards, but support and representation at work. Years of anxiety and insecurity have taken their toll on membership. The so-called 'AA fourth emergency' model of unionism, delivering services and benefits to a largely passive membership, has patently failed to deliver growth. As one union official commented wryly: 'You can't tell a worker who's scared to join a union because it means risking the sack – don't worry, we offer a wonderful discount holiday scheme'.

Louise Chinnery agrees that the 'AA' approach doesn't work: 'In Covent Garden we didn't sell the benefits of joining a union. We listened. They told us what their problems are – they haven't got a contract, the tips system is grossly unfair, low pay and poor health and safety... If we hadn't listened we'd never have known. Only then could we arm people with information and help them organise for the rights they need'.

Concern about the hard sell are not confined to the sharp end of the jobs market. Dawn Butler, a 27 year-old organiser fired more by her experience of discrimination as a black woman than any family back-

ground in the union movement, is organising private sector profes-
sional workers in the computer industry. According to Dawn: 'There's
this thing going around that we have to find out what product trade
unionism is and how to market it. But you either believe in it [trade
unionism] or you don't. It's a not a commodity, we are not like a
hoover. We're about solidarity and you can't sell that – you offer it'.

As Britain's largest democratic voluntary organisation, the future
success of the trade union movement depends critically on the confidence and active involvement of its members. That means that unions
also need to take a hard look at how they organise themselves.

Union cultures which have developed around the needs and interests of middle-aged men in full-time steady jobs are not always best
suited to the needs of the new workforce of the 1990s. The 'like recruits
like' principle is second nature to many of the new generation of organisers, but women, young, and black people are still under-represented
among both paid and unpaid union activists. Union officials who
submerge themselves in the union movement, at the expense of family
commitments and a life outside, risk getting out of touch with the very
people they aim to represent.

The TUC Youth Forum has voiced explicitly the need for less
bureaucratic committees and more networks, less conferences more
events, and less talk and more action. Louise Chinnery stresses the
importance of new informal action-based forms of organisation to
involve young workers: 'It's not a bureaucratic structural thing meeting at union head quarters. We meet when we're out leafleting on the
streets. But now we have to find a way of feeding our ideas up through
the union'. While union conservatives may question the 'guerilla
theatre' tactics of the Covent Garden campaign, Louise is clear that it
has two key aims: first to organise new members and second to involve
existing ones. Arguably, the campaign's in your face style holds a good
deal more appeal for young activists than sitting on stuffy committees.

There are signs that unions are beginning to respond to the challenge
to reinvent themselves and develop new, participative forms of organisation such as the Covent Garden campaign and *interActiv*. Mark
Holding comments: 'There's more activity among young people in
unions than there's been for some time. There's a bit of space around.
But there aren't enough of us yet. Unless we talk to each other and
support each other there's a danger we'll all burn out and go off in
different directions'.

The pressure is intense on any newly self-organised group to reach the parts the rest of the union movement has failed to reach. The new generation of young organisers want to be strategic. According to Mark: 'We have to make choices about where we're going right down to whether we should be given the job of going out into schools. It's a mammoth task. It would be putting the cart before the horse. We need to start with young workers in the workplace first.'

More unions are looking to organise young workers and take on young organisers to do the job, but inevitably this can lead to inter-generational friction. As one young organiser put it: 'They [older trade unionists] have got knowledge and experience and we want to tap it. But we want power through that. It means them letting go of some of their status and power.' Another goes further: 'I'll have failed in my job if the generation after us have to put up with what I've had to.' If unions fail to embrace deeper cultural change, there is a danger that young workers will vote with their feet. In the words of one young activist: 'We've got to be allowed to win sometimes – and fail some-times. If we keep banging our head against a brick wall we'll walk away and try something else.'

Dawn Butler recognises the frustration felt by many of the new recruits but her sense of commitment keeps her going: 'People need to start listening. We know what we want, but it's a struggle. If I didn't really believe in unions I'd have given up but this is my mission in life.'

The experience isn't new. The roots of the New Unionism campaign are to be found in the first wave of New Unionism at the end of the last century (when the union movement transformed itself from a club for the largely male and older privileged few into a mass social movement open to all). Young workers played a leading role in that upsurge of popular unionism. At the height of the Great Dock Strike, Ben Tillet was just 29 and Will Thorne only 32. The leaders of the match girls' strike – Alice France, Kate Slater and Mary Driscoll – were teenagers.

But there is one crucial difference. The first wave New Unionists had the advantage of starting with a clean slate. Mark Holding explains: 'The original new unionists didn't have to work through old structures and try to change them. They just set up new unions. But we can't start from scratch. We have to change what we've got and that's a daunting process.'

Rejuvenation has to be the name of the new union game. But first unions need to rediscover their idealism. The been-there-done-that (and it didn't work then) scepticism which imbues parts of the union movement does little to inspire the new organisers. Mark again: 'There are too many people still working for unions who've lost their belief. There's too much cynicism. We need the sense that we're going somewhere – some urgency.'

If the union movement can crack the challenge of organising young workers, there's a good chance it can also crack the broader challenge of rejuvenation. Replenishing the ranks of young trade unionists requires a new level of experimentation and innovation. As an activist on the TUC youth forum pointed out, unlike women and black people, young workers don't retain their identity forever, they don't stay young. The challenge of winning the involvement of young people in unions is constantly up for renewal. And implementing the necessary changes to capture the imagination of each new wave of young workers, by its very nature, has to be rapid.

While a change of government is no guarantee of growth, there is growing confidence that unions can organise their way out of decline and so help build social and economic solidarity and justice. The new government's commitment to boost jobs for the young and devolve power is welcome. But the drive to deepen democracy and develop citizenship cannot stop at the workplace door. Through unions, young people can develop a strong voice and help shape strategies which genuinely enhance working lives.

New Unionism can help create the space young workers need to make a real contribution. But if it is to succeed, others must be ready to make room for the 'us generation'; let them make their own mistakes and score their own victories. The stakes are high for young workers and unions alike. If unions get it right, organising workers looks set to become the cause for a whole new generation.

Underworked and underpaid

Ian Brinkley

What has happened to youth unemployment and employment is a key test of whether the previous government's strategy of labour market deregulation worked. The under 25s have in many ways borne the full brunt of the removal and weakening of employment protections, cuts in welfare benefits, and the decline of trade union organisation and membership. If deregulation had worked, young people should have done better than the national average in the mid 1990s compared with the mid 1980s.

Are young people doing better or worse than the average?

The evidence shows that far from doing better than the average, the relative position of the under 25s has worsened in the 1990s. The chart below shows ILO unemployment rates from spring 1984 to spring 1997 (1984 is the earliest year for which ILO unemployment rates on a consistent definition are available). Two conclusions can be drawn:

- Firstly, the gap between the unemployment rate for all ages and the unemployment rate for the under 25s seems to be greater in the mid 1990s than in the mid 1980s. In other words, compared to the national average, young people are doing worse.
- Secondly, the differences between youth rates and the national rate narrowed in the 1980s labour market recovery. There has been no narrowing in the unemployment rate in the 1990s recovery.

These conclusions are not significantly affected by the inclusion or exclusion of young people combining full time education and work –

the idea that the overall picture might be distorted by an increase in the number of students flooding the jobs market in search of part time work does not seem to be true.

Chart 1: Under 25s Unemployment

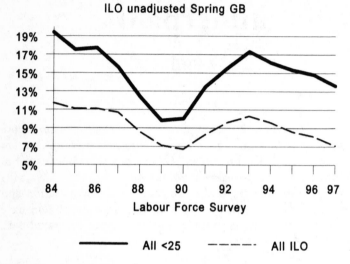

ILO unadjusted Spring GB

Labour Force Survey

——— All <25   – – – – – All ILO

Chart 2: Youth Unemployment Compared

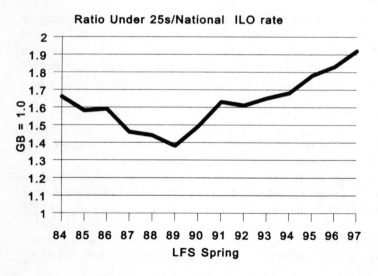

Ratio Under 25s/National ILO rate

LFS Spring

The difference between youth and national rates can be more clearly shown as a ratio. For under 25s the unemployment rate in spring 1987 was 15.6 per cent against a national average of 10.7 per cent, so that youth unemployment was 1.46 times the national average. In spring 1997 the unemployment rate for under 25s was 13.6 per cent against 7.1 per cent for the national average, so that youth unemployment was 1.92 times the national average. This is shown in the chart which compares the unemployment rate for under 25s and all ILO unemployed between spring 1984 and spring 1997.

Young men and women compared

Younger men in particular suffer from very high ILO unemployment rates and their relative position has worsened significantly since the mid 1980s. In spring 1987 the unemployment rate for young men under 25 was 1.38 times the national average, but in spring 1997 it was 2.2 times the national average.

Younger women had similar unemployment rates to young men in the mid 1980s but have since done less badly. By spring 1997 unemployment among young women was 11 per cent, compared with a male under 25 unemployment rate of nearly 16 per cent.

Younger women have also seen a deterioration in their relative unemployment position compared with the national average, but the deterioration has been by much less than for young men. In spring 1987 the ratio between young women's unemployment rate and the national average was 1.35 times, but by spring 1997 this had increased to 1.55 times

The lower unemployment rates for young women, compared with young men, and the lower ratio between young women's unemployment rate and the national average, is partly due to the general improvement in women's employment rates over the past decade.

However, when the unemployment rates for young men are compared with the overall male unemployment rate and the unemployment rates for young women are compared with overall unemployment rates for women, then the differences between the sexes largely disappears (see chart 3).

In other words, when young women are compared with the female average unemployment rate, they are doing just as badly, relatively speaking, as when young men are compared with the male average unemployment rate.

Chart 3: Unemployment Ratio by Sex 1984–96

Ratio <25 male/female rate to average male/female rate

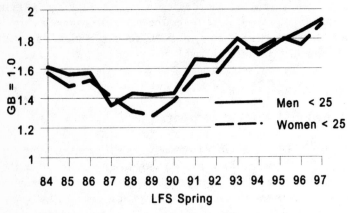

LFS Spring

Fewer young people competing for work

The worsening position of young people compared with the national average also took place despite a major decline in the numbers of young people competing for work. Between spring 1989 and spring 1997 the total population of under 25s fell from 7.6 million to 6.2 million, a drop of 19 per cent. Over the same period the proportion in full time education increased from 20 per cent to 37 per cent.

The numbers active in the labour market (in work or looking for work, including students) fell from 6.1 million to 4.4 million, a fall of 28 per cent. If those in full time education are excluded, the fall in the total numbers active was from 5.5 million to 3.4 million, a drop of 39 per cent (see chart 4).

A fall in the supply of labour on this scale should have seen the labour market position of young people improve significantly. Indeed, in the late 1980s there were serious worries that the so-called demographic timebomb' would result in widespread labour shortages in industries traditionally reliant on recruiting large numbers of young people. But as can be seen above, the reverse has happened: the unemployment position of young people compared with adults has worsened.

Chart 4: Fewer Young people in 1990s

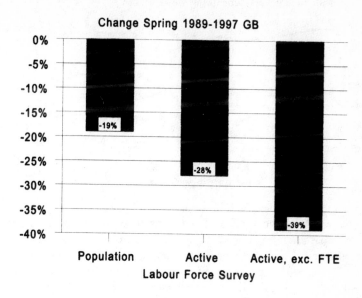

Change Spring 1989-1997 GB

Young people's relative pay falls

If the free market economic orthodoxy was right, then a fall in the hourly earnings of young people would make them cheaper relative to other workers, firms would demand more of them, and their unemployment rate would fall relative to the national average. Conversely, if young people became relatively more expensive than older workers, then firms would hire fewer of them and their unemployment would rise compared to the national average.

Earnings data from the New Earnings Survey shows the opposite has happened. The earnings measure is full time gross average hourly earnings – including overtime – for those on adult rates, Great Britain, April of each year. Between April 1984 and April 1996 hourly earnings for young men fell from 82.8 per cent of the average to 72.8 per cent, while for young women hourly earnings fell from 70.5 per cent of the average to 65.8 per cent. This is shown in chart 5. Yet despite these falls the unemployment position of young people worsened when compared against the national average.

43

Chart 5: Young people's relative pay

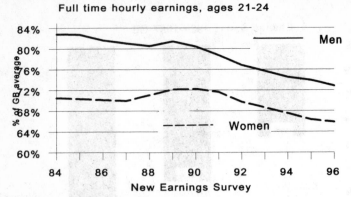

Full time hourly earnings, ages 21-24

The same pattern emerges if hourly earnings of young men are compared with the average for all men and if the hourly earnings of young women are compared with the average for all women. This is shown in chart 6. Yet despite the fall in relative pay for both young men and young women, young men fared worse than all men and young women fared worse than all women in terms of unemployment.

Chart 6: Male and female pay compared

males/females ages 21-24 as % of male/female average

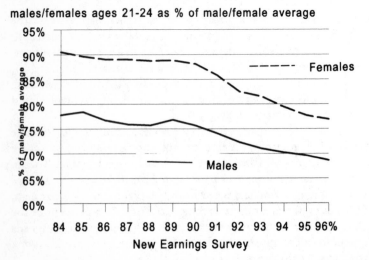

Chart 7: New Jobs mainly Part time & Temporary

Employees GB Spring 1993-97

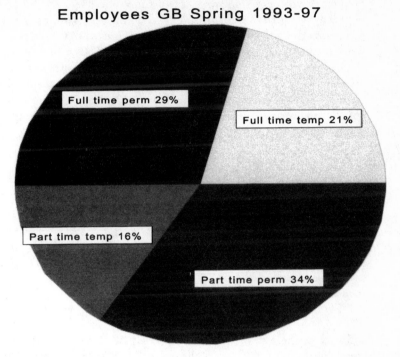

Full time perm 29%

Full time temp 21%

Part time temp 16%

Part time perm 34%

Young people and the recovery

One reason for the fall in both relative earnings and a worsening of the relative unemployment position of young people is the quality of job creation in this recovery, and the sort of jobs young people are often forced to take. The household Labour Force Survey shows that comparing 1990 and 1997 the economy still had 660,000 fewer full time employee jobs and 680,000 more part time employee jobs.

Moreover, there has been a remarkable increase in temporary work over the recession and into the first years of the recovery. The balance is now changing, with more full time and permanent jobs coming through as confidence in the recovery grows. But even so, only 29 per cent of the net increase in employment between spring 1993 and spring 1997 has been in permanent, full time work (see chart 7).

The lack of full time permanent jobs has meant that the 1990s have

seen a rapid increase in the numbers of people in part time or temporary work who say they want a full time job. The LFS shows that
between spring 1990 and spring 1997 the numbers working part time
in a main job (including the self-employed) but who wanted full time
work increased by over 120 per cent, from 350,000 or 6.3 per cent of
all part time workers to 780,000 or 12.2 per cent of all part time workers. The numbers in temporary work who want a permanent job has
risen by 97 per cent, increasing from 330,000 in Spring 1990 to
650,000 in Spring 1997 or 39 per cent of all those in temporary
employment.

FIGURE 8: INVOLUNTARY PART TIME AND TEMPORARY WORKING INCREASES

Spring GB unadjusted 000s	Spring 1990	Spring 1992	Spring 1997
Part time, want full time work	350	670	780
Temporary, want permanent work	330*	430	650

* may not be directly comparable with later estimates. Part time is employees
& self-employed.
Source: Labour Force Survey

Many of these new jobs are very low paid. Nearly 50 per cent of
'entry jobs' which are filled by the unemployed and new entrants to the
labour force paid less than £4 an hour, and 25 per cent paid less than £3
an hour. Many of the jobs which young people take are likely to be
very low paid indeed.

The latest New Earnings Survey provides information on the pay
of full time men and women and part time women workers by age
group for April 1996. The NES shows that in April 1996 hourly
median earnings (the median is the level at which exactly half earn
more and half earn less) for full time male employees aged 21-24 was
£5.72 an hour.

By contrast, males between 18 and 20 had median earnings of £4.13
an hour. The corresponding figures for female full time workers were
£5.37 an hour and £4.04 an hour respectively. Female part time employees aged 21-24 had median earnings of £3.83 an hour, female part timers
ages 18-20 had median earnings of £3.61 an hour. Earnings were much
lower down the scale. The hourly earnings for those in the bottom 10
per cent and bottom 25 per cent are set out below in figure 9.

FIGURE 9: HOURLY EARNINGS OF UNDER 25S IN 1995

Ages 21-24	Lowest 10%	Lowest 25%
Males Full time	£3.75 or less	£4.50 or less
Females Full time	£3.50 or less	£4.26 or less
Women Part time	£2.86 or less	£3.30 or less
Ages 18-20		
Males Full time	£2.75 or less	£3.41 or less
Females Full time	£2.86 or less	£3.39 or less
Women Part time	£2.82 or less	£3.25 or less

Note: all figures gross hourly earnings including overtime, GB, April 1995. NES estimates of hourly earnings for part time males by age not available.
Source: New Earnings Survey

Chart 10: The sort of jobs the unemployed want

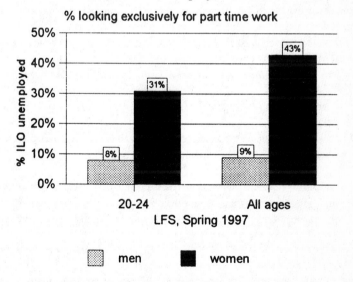

% looking exclusively for part time work

LFS, Spring 1997

Temporary and part time work may offer opportunities for students and young people who do not want a permanent job, but most of those under 25 are likely to be looking for full time jobs. Indeed, the Labour Force Survey shows that in spring 1997 only 16 per cent of those aged

47

20-24 who were ILO unemployed were looking exclusively for part time work, compared with 21 per cent of all ILO unemployed. However, there was a significant difference between men and women – only 8 per cent of unemployed young men ages 20-24 were looking exclusively for part time work.

It is hard to avoid the conclusion that many young people, and especially young men, face the same problems as many other workers in the labour markets of the 1990s. Although the balance is now changing as the recovery matures, since 1993 most of the net rise in employment has so far come from part time, temporary work and many of the 'entry' jobs into the workforce are very low paid indeed. The mismatch between the sort of jobs people want, and those available, is ensuring that many of those who do get a foothold in the labour market are in jobs they do not really want to be in.

Solutions and options

The worsening position of young people in the labour market is not confined to the UK. The Organisation for Economic Co-operation and Development (OECD) has looked at the issue of youth unemployment across a wide range of industrialised economies in the *Employment Outlook*, published in June 1996. This confirmed that many of the changes identified in the employment position – despite falls in relative wages and a decline in supply – are taking place in other economies.

The OECD suggests two reasons. One is that youth unemployment is very sensitive to overall economic conditions:

> As long as total unemployment remains high, it is unrealistic to expect a significant improvement in youth job prospects: both the employment and unemployment rates of young people are highly responsive to the overall state of the labour market.
>
> (OECD *Employment Outlook*, 1996)

Youth unemployment must be tackled as part of a wider commitment to full employment, and investment in people. A sustained recovery in the labour market will see more full time permanent jobs created. A recovery accompanied by investment in the social infrastructure – in social housing and urban regeneration – and by large scale work and training programmes targeted on the long term unemployed are needed and will help to ensure the sustainability of the recovery.[1]

The second reason suggested by the OECD is that as demand in the industrialised economies shifts towards more skilled and experienced workers, the young – and especially those without qualifications – are being left behind. Firms are preferring somewhat older and more experienced workers, even though younger workers are much cheaper. There is certainly evidence that in the UK unemployment is exceptionally low among well educated workers in the 25-34 age group (and much higher among those with less educational qualifications in the same age group).

The UK experience certainly contradicts the view that deregulation works, and the OECD study confirms that there is no evidence that minimum wages or employment protection legislation has adversely affected the labour market position of those most at risk, such as the unskilled and young people. According to the OECD;

> Although economic theory indicates that wage floors can price low skills workers out of jobs, employment and unemployment rates for youth, women and unskilled workers do not appear to be significantly correlated with the incidence of the low paid employment.

What is very clear is that the labour market 'reform' since 1980 have produced an almost unique increase in wage inequality in the UK economy compared with the rest of Europe, leaving the UK the low pay capital of Europe in terms of the number of low paid jobs. The loss of minimum wage protection, job security, the weakening of trade unions and the loss and reduction of welfare benefits have all contributed to this unfortunate distinction. For young people, especially those without qualifications, the social costs of these measures have been severe.

The new government has inherited a difficult and deteriorating labour market position for young people, and especially for those leaving school without qualifications. Improvements in both vocational training and education are badly needed alongside labour market and investment measures targeted on those groups and communities which have not benefitted significantly from the general economic recovery.

The New Deal for young claimants is an important first step in tackling the problems of youth unemployment, as is the present overhaul of policies on youth training and the transition from school to work.

The introduction of a minimum wage will clearly benefit disproportionately many young people in low paid work today, and without
adversely affecting their employment prospects.[2] The implementation
of EU social policy and the proposal for fairer employment protections
and rights to be set out in the forthcoming White Paper will also help
reduce exploitation and encourage more efficient employment practices in the 'bargain basement' of the labour market. There is now
scope for significant progress, especially if the general economic recovery is sustained. And among the key indicators of success will be the
reversal of the trend of the past decade towards higher relative youth
unemployment and lower relative youth wages.

*This article draws on the Labour Force Survey, an official household
survey which uses definitions set down by the International Labour
Organisation. Unemployment is defined as looking for work in the four
weeks before the survey and being able to start a job in two weeks time.
Employment is one hour of work a week, and includes those in full time
education. Young people usually refers to the under 25s. Unless otherwise stated, all figures are for Great Britain.*

Notes

1. The 1996 & 1997 TUC Budget Submissions set out some proposal in this
   area.
2. *Arguments for a Minimum Wage*, TUC 1995.

A new deal for young black Britain

Balbir Chatrik

Mention youth training to many people and they are likely to be indifferent or dismiss it as a cynical exercise in cheap labour. With its connotations of an industrial army, training has a poor image yet it forms the central part of Labour's manifesto commitment to the young and long-term unemployed. The budget of July 1997 earmarked £3.9bn for the full Welfare to Work initiative; of this £3,150m has been allocated to the New Deal programme, which started in April 1998. Designed to get 250,000 18-24 year olds into work, its training schemes will provide a crucial period of transition in the lives of hundreds of thousands of young people. In particular it will effect the lives of a disproportionately large number of young Black British and British Asian men and women. Race is a significant issue in the New Deal.

Two of the main features of the labour market during the last twenty years have been the rise in youth unemployment and the rapid increase in young people remaining in post-compulsory full time education. In 1994 the proportion of young people staying on in post-compulsory education was 50 per cent; two years later, it had risen to 73 per cent. Between 1984 and 1996, the number of 16 and 17 year olds in employment fell by over 25 per cent to 318,000. As Ian Brinkley points out in this book, the rate of youth unemployment has been significantly higher than the rate for adults (in autumn 1997, the unemployment rate for 16-19 year olds was 17 per cent, compared to 13 per cent for 18-24 year olds, and 8 per cent for the all age population). The deregulation of the labour market has had the effect of extending the period of young's people dependency on their parents (64 per cent of 16-24 year

51

olds live with their parents). The Conservative government sought to institutionalise this trend. In 1988 Nicholas Scott, then minister for social security, withdrew benefits for 16 and 17 year olds. In 1990 Youth Training replaced the Youth Training Scheme. The government proclaimed a YT Guarantee, promising a place on the new scheme for all unemployed 16-17 year olds. Participants were given a training allowance which could be topped up by employers or trainers: 16 year olds received £29.50 (£30.00 from April 1997), those over 17 received £35.00. Unemployed 16 and 17 year olds were compelled to enter YT or risk an immediate loss of benefit.

This element of compulsion established in Youth Training was carried over into the Jobseeker's Allowance, which was introduced in October 1996. The element of conscription in YT and the implementing of sanctions against those who dropped out of training or who refused to join, resulted in the impoverishment and homelesness of many young people.[1]

The latest figures show that of the 149,000 unemployed young people, 127,400 have form of state income; 85 per cent of the young unemployed are without any visible, legal means of support.[2] The YT guarantee of a training place for all was a failure. According to the Department for Education and Employment, 47 per cent of all young people left YT before completion.[3] The YT Laver's Survey conducted by the department revealed that one in five were unhappy with the training on offer, and 21 per cent had left because of the poor rates of pay.[4] Despite this, the Labour government's New Deal extends the element of compulsion to include 18-24 year olds.

The New Deal offers the young unemployed four options. The first and most attractive is a job with an employer. Businesses which participate will receive a subsidy – per individual – of £60 per week for six months. An extra £750 per placement will be given to provide the equivalent of one day a week structured learning that leads to a vocational qualification. The assumption has been made that 40 per cent of those entering the New Deal will chose this option. The second option allows young people without basic educational qualifications to study or train, whilst on benfit, for up to six months. The third option is six months' work experience in the voluntary sector, with one day per week of structured education or training. Voluntary organisations will receive a fee of £3,200 per six month placement, whilst trainees receive their benefits plus a £400 grant. This option is intended to make a contribution to the national objective of training 50,000 child care workers. The fourth option is designed to meet the government's aim of improving the employability of young people through community projects, in particular those associated with energy conservation. Similar to option three, young people will receive their benefit plus a £400 grant.

The focus of the New Deal on the 18-24 year olds theatens the already precarious position of under 18 year olds in the labour market. A separate programme, called target 2000 has been set up, aimed at 16 and 17 year olds who are not in education, employment or on a training programme. The intention of Target 200 is to increase their skills levels and help reintegrate them into the labour market, through a number of different schemes. The National Traineeships, recommended in the Dearing report, will be implemented. New Start is designed to keep 14-19 year olds in some form of learning, for all 16 and 17 year olds, whether they are in work or on a training programme. Speaking at the Modern Apprenticeship National Conference in June 1997 Labour Minister Baroness Blackstone said the scheme, 'aims to raise the number of young people by the age of 18 who have achieved or are working towards an NVQ level 2 or equivalent, and key skills'. Target 2000 received its full scale launch with the introduction of the Education Bill at the end of 1997.

When New Labour first made its pledge to end youth unemployment in November 1995, the number of claimants aged 18-24 who had been out work for longer than six months was 241,000. In early 1996 numbers started to rise; since then they have begun to fall quite dramatically. The April 1997 claimants' statistics show that unemployment among 18-24 year olds who had been out of work for longer than six months stood at 171,600. Nevertheless every month the 10,000 young people who pass the six months unemployment threshold are added to this figure. The strategy of the New Deal is to divert this monthly flow and to begin reducing the numbers of those least employable, and who will need the most help. This phase of the New Deal should be seen as an 'employability' initiative rather than simply as job creation.

18-24 year olds who have been unemployed for more than six months are a significantly disavantaged population. 50 per cent of them have been unemployed for more than one and a half years.[5] 73 per cent are young men, and a quarter are concentrated in just 18 of Britain's 471 local authority areas. Their social exclusion from mainstream society leaves them cynical of civic authority and wary of all forms of bureaucracy. They will be the litmus test of New Deal's openness to youth cultures and to its ability to revive the thwarted hopes and aspirations of a generation of young people. In particular the response of this pool of disaffected young people will indicate how far the New Deal has been able to challenge racial discrimination. Black young people are disproportionately represented amongst the long-term unemployed. About 30,000, or 13 per cent, of the 18-24 year olds who have been unemployed for six months or more are Black. They form only 8 per cent of the 18-24 year olds who have jobs.[6]

The unemployment rate for Black 16-24 year olds is 22 per cent. The rate for African-Caribbeans is 34 per cent, compared to 28 per cent for Pakistani and Bangladeshi young men and 20 per cent for Indians.[7] The majority of young Black unemployed are concentrated in 18 of Britain's 471 local authority areas. In the London Borough of Kensington and Chelsea, unemployment amongst the Black group is 70 per cent, compared with 6 per cent for the comparable White group. In Tower Hamlets in London there are 4,000 Black unemployed 16-24 year olds, compared to only 500 White 16-24 year olds.[8] Racial discrimination not only denies young Black British people employment opportunities, but also influences the type of jobs they eventually obtain. They are more likely to be employed in jobs which have poor terms and conditions, lower pay and less security of tenure. They are less likely to be on a training scheme based with an employer. Black organisations are concerned that Black young people will not gain access to the better opportunities with employers under the New Deal. Kanchan Jadeja, the director of Sia, an umbrella organisation for the Black voluntary sector, reiterated this point when she wrote in *Community Care* magazine that Black young people 'may have less suitable offers under the scheme, which will offer training and work to long term unemployed young people and not help with any discrimination they may face'.[9]

Research into the experiences of Black, young, job seekers suggests that racial discrimination (intentional and unintentional) remains a major factor affecting their work and training opportunities. In a recent study by the Commission for Racial Equality, job applications from both Black and White applicants were submitted to prospective employers. Their survey revealed 'clear statistical evidence of [racial discrimination] when jobs were advertised in newspapers and journals'.[10] Research carried out by the Haringey Employment Commission in 1997, in the London Borough of Haringey, listed a number of examples of indirect discrimination.[11] Employers with predominantly White workforces perpetuated their ethnic composition by relying on word of mouth to recruit new staff. The Commission found a reluctance amongst employers to interview or employ people from particular post code areas. And the lack of Black employees in senior positions within organisations contributed to an overall sense that young Black people were not welcome.

Young people interviewed in the research confirmed that racism was 'one of the principal barriers to their participation in the labour market'. As one young person reported, 'I've been looking for work for two years. As soon as I walk through the door for an interview that's it, they've already made up their minds. They think things like, 'he's a bit dark' or 'he looks a bit aggressive'. Another, 'Mark' described one of his experiences: 'I went for a job at a DIY shop. I said I had three years experience. They said come for an interview and told me I was the last one to be interviewed. I went there and he saw me and said he had one more interview and he looked really promising. I could tell though he was surprised when he saw I was Black.' The Commission found similar problems in the Borough's Education and Careers Service: 'Some teachers have difficulty dealing with students from poorer or diverse ethnic backgrounds because of limited understanding of other cultures, leading to low teacher expectations'.

There are a number of general concerns about how the New Deal is going to affect young people. Employers may try to profit from the system of subsidies by substituting or displacing other workers. Not only may the New Deal have a negative impact on the under 18s, there is the possibility that employers may substitute 18–24 year olds when the higher subsidy of £75 a week applies to those aged over 25 and unemployed for two years. While sanctions against abusive employers have not been emphasised, the Government has made it clear that the New Deal will operate sanctions against young people – using the JSA regulations. Those who refuse all four options without good cause, will have their benefit suspended for a period of two weeks. If, after adjudication, they still refuse to join an option, their benefit will be stopped for a further four week period. Each young person will be expected to have a case worker, responsible for 'ensuring that young people do not simply "drop off" the programme at the end of the funded period'.

The experience of youth training has proved that this form of compulsion is unlikely to work. By confusing the delivery of training and employment opportunities with the means to gaining an income, YT not only created great difficulties for dissatisfied young people but discredited itself. As one woman told Youthaid, 'I don't want no government saying you haven't had a job since year so we're going to send you on a hairdressing course. I'm saving up £1,300 to do a sound engineering diploma. Why should I do hairdressing instead? Maybe they should pay me to do what I want.'[12] Sanctions are justified on the grounds that young people are said to be indifferent to training. Nevertheless the great majority of young people want opportunities in their lives. They will volunteer for schemes which can enhance their prospects and which will encourage their personal aspirations. Sanctions may well end up penalising young people for the poor quality of training on offer. In both these instances of possible employer exploitation and use of sanctions, racial discrimination is likely to be a significant issue. Youth Training was a case in point. The scheme provided preparatory training, which was often used to provide short 'taster' courses for young people overdue a YT place. When it was used simply as a means of meeting the YT Guarantee, preparatory training was a holding tank with very little to offer. Department of Education and Employment statistics revealed that between 70 and 80 per cent of young people on these preparatory courses were Black, while only 30 per cent to 40 per cent of mainstream trainees were Black.[13] The YT Leavers' Survey found that 64 per cent of White young people got a job on leaving YT, compared to 40 per cent of African-Caribbeans and 39 per cent of Asians.

The New Deal Task Force set up to implement the schemes has declared that it wants to ensure that 'the New Deal meets the needs of ethnic minorities'.[14] It is keen to ensure that providers of the New Deal in local areas have equality of access, specialist caseworkers and mentors. It is a hopeful sign that Black organisations and individuals have been included in both the Task Force and the Advisory Group to the Task Force. In place of the YT's preparatory training, the New Deal will operate a Gateway, a first entry point for participants, which will provide advice, guidance and individual assessment for up to four months before referral to one of the four options. The Employment Service will invite local consortia to run the Gateways. These are likely to include the Careers Service, hostels, voluntary organisations in the alcohol and drugs field, and the probation and social services. A number of critics are concerned that they will be located in Job Centres, which are associated in the minds of many as threatening and unsympathetic places.[15]

It is hoped that Black organisations will be involved in the local consortia. The higher rate of Black unemployment will mean that the young Black people are more likely to be directed to take up off under the New Deal programme. Its success will depend not only on ensuring equal access for Black young people to all options, but perhaps even more, on the resolution of wider social and economic discrimination against Black young people.

Notes

1. I. Maclagen, *Four Years Severe Hardship*, Youthaid and Barnardo's, 1993.
2. See Balbir Chatrik, *New Deal – Fair Deal? Black Young People in the Labour Market*, Barnardo's, The Children Society and Youthaid, 1997.
3. *Government Supported Training, Statistical Bulletin*, DfEE 1997.
4. Chatrik, *op.cit.*
5. D. Simmons, P. Convey, T. Bewick, *Making the New Deal Work*, Training and Employment Network 1997.
6. *Ibid.*
7. *Labour Force Survey*, Winter 1996/97.
8. *Labour Force Survey*, 1995/96.
9. Kanchan Jadeja, *Community Care*, 7 August 1997.
10. *We Regret to Inform You...*, CRE 1996.
11. *Tackling Unemployment – Learning from Haringey*, Haringey Employment Commission 1997.
12. Chatrik, *op.cit.*
13. *Review of Arrangements to Manage and Monitor the YT Gurantee*, DfEE 1996.
14. New Deal Task Force, September 1997.
15. See for example Stuart Fleming, 'The deal makers', in *New Statesman*, 3 October 1997.

Bypassing politics? A critical look at DiY culture

Peter Gartside

Although there are problems in treating the various strands of DiY culture/Non-Violent Direct Action (NVDA) protest as some kind of unified 'movement', affiliations and solidarities clearly exist. The solidarity between different strands was cemented by their common opposition to, and victimisation by, the Criminal Justice and Public Order Act (1994). Amongst other things, the CJA hit at 'DiY'/Rave culture, at 'new age' travelling, squatting, and at NVDA as a way of doing politics. An informal network of activists and campaigns now exists with its own relatively sophisticated 'underground' media covering the range of DiY culture from within its own ranks.[1] DiY culture does not conform to what has been called 'single issue' politics; a variety of concerns interact and overlap in complex ways. (Later I will suggest ways in which a possibly useful internal differentiation can be made.) DiY culture is also more than what is understood generally as a 'youth sub-culture', a (commodified) *style*. It is right to think of it as a 'culture', an emergent 'structure of feeling'. I don't attempt a comprehensive survey of DiY/NVDA culture; such a thing would be impossible. My analysis is necessarily partial and I recognise that I leave out a great deal.

To generalise for a moment, I think it fair to say that this is a type of 'politics' most readily identified with, or supported by, young people. There is, of course, a danger of overstating the importance of direct action politics, of extrapolating from the amount of coverage these colourful and eminently photogenic protests have received.

Committed activism is a minority, and localised, pursuit among young(ish) people. But beyond a core of activists, DiY culture has touched and influenced many others. This is the politics of the 'Thatcher generation', of those who grew up in the period when the ideas and institutions of collectivism and social welfarism - even the notion of 'society' - came under radical attack. DiY culture is in some senses a reaction to the individualistic and acquisitive culture Thatcherism promoted. The 'DiY' ethic has nothing to do with neo-Victorian 'self-help' individualism: it would be more accurate to call it a Do-it-*Ourselves* culture, a collective resistance to commodified culture. For example, the strands of dance/drug culture with which the movement is entwined are consciously opposed to the commodification of that culture exemplified by the superclubs (e.g. Ministry of Sound, Cream) and licensed mega-raves like Tribal Gathering. It is making your own fun, rather than buying into it, which is important.

DiY culture is the protest of people who have borne the brunt of the New Right onslaught on welfare and civil liberties, but also of those for whom this is an informed, reflexive choice: a 'life politics'. This has made for a sometimes uneasy alliance and some confused analyses. Finally, it is also the politics of a generation for whom the language and the theoretical debates of the left are, generally speaking, a foreign tongue. DiY culture is to some extent a politics of the depoliticised New Labour era.

Political culture de-politicised

If one thing might be said to unite DiY/NVDA culture it is an explicit rejection - or bypassing - of organised party politics (and of environmental pressure groups); a suspicion that 'all' politicians are duplicitous, corrupt and remote from DiY culture's key concerns (A30 tunneller Muppet Dave's *Guardian* questionnaire: Q: How will you vote in the next election? A: I won't; don't trust any of them).[2] Hence the emphasis on *direct* action, doing it *yourself*. With the emphasis on action there is also a resistance to, perhaps suspicion of, the articulation of coherent 'theory': a certain defiant anti-intellectualism (the way Swampy - having, for who knows what reason, agreed to appear - mumbled and grinned his way through the programme 'Have I Got News for You' is symptomatic).

Disenchantment with representative politics, with politicians, with what is seen as the serving of 'ideology' or 'vested interests', is widespread in contemporary culture and is, I think, one reason why DiY culture has gained a sort of low-level, and seemingly increasing, support from non-participants. Thus, while the left-liberal media - e.g. the *Guardian*, *New Statesman* - has long championed DiY activism (in an uncritical way which this essay seeks to challenge), what used to be designated the 'Tory' press has recently joined in. This might initially seem puzzling: *Swampy* feted in the *Sunday Express*?! Possibly it only amounts to a temporary fascination with the '(anti-) style' of colourful NVDA figures rather than with the specific aims of the protests. Once emptied of content there is nothing contentious or 'political' about celebrating values like 'commitment', 'integrity' and 'idealism' ('fanaticism' would be a different matter). At a deeper level, this positive mainstream coverage of DiY/NVDA illustrates just how widespread disillusion with/disengagement from representative politics has become.

The cynicism with which representative politics is viewed needs to be theorised and historicised rather than described in terms of some sort of millenarian 'end of politics'. This is something Timothy Bewes does brilliantly in his *Cynicism and Postmodernity*, a book which has influenced my thoughts here.[3] To be sure, there is plenty wrong with politics as it is practised: trivially adversarial, media- and soundbite-led, centralised, archaic, fatally over-reliant for its legitimation on the ideal of 'economic growth'. Under the circumstances many people quite rightly feel unrepresented. But 'politics' and 'political' have lately become pejoratives. It appears that no-one wants to defend the idea of politics as a commitment to an ideology, as precisely the representation of some interests against others. Symptomatically, in the realm of theory, various versions of the 'end of politics', or a search for a politics 'beyond left and right', or a new 'post-scarcity' order have been proposed.

It is difficult not to be swept along by this wave of 'end-ism'. I remember feeling something of the same at the anti-Criminal Justice Bill march/rally in Hyde Park, October 1994. Some of us were respectfully listening to the platform speakers - 'old' Labour, SWP, Liberty - when we became aware that behind us a rave party was getting under way. A sound-system on the back of a truck had somehow made its way up Park Lane, pumping out the soon to be criminalised 'repetitive beats'. For an instant there was a tension: should we stay here - the speakers themselves were beginning to get repetitive - or go and have a dance? As I like to remember it, significant numbers at that moment turned their backs on the platform and went to join the 'DiY' carnival. At the time it seemed a massively significant moment; on reflection it would be unwise to suggest there has been some final, radical shift in the nature of 'radical' politics. The millenarian impulse to declare the 'end' of things (socialism, politics, history) should be resisted (the former is arguably only over to the extent that the word 'socialism' has been expunged from the political vocabulary). The tendency, as Timothy Bewes points out, has been to misrepresent (reify) a temporary state of affairs as *the* (permanent) 'postmodern condition'. For some a terminal, cynical-ironic quietism seems the only 'position' left to take. If such an idea can be allowed, I read this kind of hyperbolic millenarian absolutism - 'all' politicians are bad, modernity and progress are *at an end* - as signs of a somewhat depressive, melancholic cultural moment.

I think Bewes is right to suggest that the party politics of the new Labour era is also implicated in this 'postmodern' suspicion of politics. Bewes argues that we have seen a de-politicisation of politics, a failure of nerve, a retreat from the notion of politics as a *risky*, visionary project. New Labour's queasiness about the word 'socialism', its anxiety not to be seen to be partisan or driven by ideology, but to be 'one nation' and inclusive (of industry as well as labour, the City as well as the public sector), not to promise anything it might not be able to deliver (and so end up promising very little) are symptomatic of the general suspicion of 'the political'.[4] The result of this, as Bewes argues powerfully, is a cultural obsession with the 'principles' of authenticity, directness, integrity, of principle itself, and a concomitant suspicion of media, mediation, 'ideology' (understood as 'dogma'), of political 'talk'; that is to say, of representation in both senses. As Bewes further argues, the logical extension of this position is a nonsensical though seductive fantasy of an untainted authentic realm beyond, or prior to, representation - ultimately a fantasy of a freedom *from* 'politics'. DiY culture - with its resistance to 'all politicians' and to anything other than direct action, and (as will be discussed below) the centrality for many activists of their concern for 'nature' - is now firmly a part of this contemporary depoliticised political scene. The NVDA stance towards 'politics' is obviously not cynical in the resigned, quietist-ironic sense. It is a more defiant *rejection*, an 'anti-theoretical, *gestural* critique'.[5] But I would argue that it is not *necessarily*, or not only, at odds with the trend towards depoliticisation.

Beyond the celebration of commitment

The discourses of DiY culture have not received the critical scrutiny they deserve. The trend has been simply to eulogise these 'grassroots' protests, to let the weary left-liberal heart be warmed by gentle young people so committed to something (*anything*) other than individualism and consumption.

Analysis from the 'left' has generally seen DiY culture as analogous to what were called the 'new social movements' - black politics, feminism, lesbian and gay activism. This implies, I think, a wilful misreading of DiY culture as a politics of 'the dispossessed'; indeed for the left this is what constitutes the 'radical'. The questionable quasi-Gramscian assumption has been that DiY culture will line up with the left because both have, ultimately, the same aims (NVDA activists only need help in realising this). The unsatisfactory confusion that was the Liverpool Dockers-cum-Reclaim the Streets rally-cum-rave in April 1997 would alone suggest otherwise.[6] Sections of the left (and ultra-left) have sought to co-opt somewhat opportunistically the undoubted energy of protest culture; sections of protest culture have been more or less keen on making these kinds of links. I hope the following discussion will explain why this project is probably doomed.

As an alternative analysis, DiY culture has been placed in a 'radical' genealogy of 'countercultures of resistance'. Variously, this is traced via anarchist-punk communes/communities, to the free festival culture of the early 1970s, or, somewhat more romantically, all the way back to seventeenth-century Diggers and Levellers and 'commoners' displaced by enclosure.[7]

The designation 'counterculture' - like 'radical', it *sounds* vaguely exciting - is one German sociologist Klaus Eder helps to theorise.[8] Although Eder is one of those carried away with the idea that class politics based on 'distributive justice' is now 'finished' (seemingly no longer necessary), and that the question of our relationship with nature is now absolutely central to politics, he analyses new forms of environmental protest in useful terms. For Eder a counterculture has always been present within modernity, indeed it is modernity (or *modernisation*) to which it is 'counter'. What distinguishes the counterculture is its radically different orientation towards 'nature'; its rejection of the technocratic, modernising assumption that 'nature' is at the service of enlightened 'man'. Throughout modernity it has sustained an often anti-rational critique of the dominant culture of industrialisation, scientific progress and economic 'growth'. The countercultural relationship with nature is essentially mystical, holistic, harmonious, even moral, rather than exploitative and instrumental. This relationship also goes beyond fundamentally utilitarian arguments for ecological 'sustainability'. The contemporary 'ecological crisis'[9] has, for Eder, intensified the importance of the counterculture; its moment has come with the growing realisation of 'the self-defeating process of modernisation'(p119). Of crucial importance is Eder's conception of this nature-loving, anti-modern and sometimes anti-rational counterculture as essentially politically ambivalent. Since dominant strains of both Left (Marxism, communism, corporatist socialism) and Right (free market capitalism, neo-liberalism) have uncritically espoused industrialisation, modernisation and growth as the keys to 'prosperity' and 'freedom', the counterculture is not naturally aligned with either. Thus it is a mistake to see radical eco-protest as intrinsically left-leaning; and not only because 'radicalism' itself is not necessarily synonymous with left politics. Eder concedes that the counterculture has sometimes manifested itself as a 'bourgeois fugitive movement' by which he means an escapist rejection of the urban and modern; it can be both anti-'progress' (scientific, technological, industrial) and politically reactionary. The merit of Eder's analysis is that it allows us to conceive of such a 'cultural movement' as 'radical' in a different way, in a different language, and to different ends than the dominant Marxist-derived tradition of radical political and cultural critique.

If we accept Eder's thesis, an English counterculture might include: the pastoral, utopian socialism of William Morris; the Edwardian 'back to the land' movement of Edward Carpenter and associated 'New Lifers'; those more recent manifestations - 'The Free Festivals and Fairs of Albion' and hippy/punk anarchist communes - which George Mackay sees as antecedents of contemporary DiY culture. But it could also encompass conservationist 'heritage' discourses; aristocratic, anti-democratic currents in neo-Malthusian 'deep ecology'; elements of what Anthony Giddens calls 'philosophic conservatism' (which he distinguishes from New Right neo-liberalism); the recent mobilisation of the pro-hunting, anti-'townie' country lobby. Aspects of DiY culture - particularly anti-road protest - can, I think, be situated within this broad, politically ambivalent, countercultural nexus.

Nature, tradition and mysticism - 'Our' English countryside

> Good people of Newbury! We, the road protestors ... are all here
> because we love the countryside of merry England. We cannot sit back
> and let our heritage be destroyed... In the true spirit of England, in the
> true spirit of our mythic heroes, King Arthur and Robyn Hood, we are
> prepared to stand up for truth and justice ... You, the people of
> Newbury, are the guardians of a noble heritage. History is written into
> the land around you ... In times of great need England has always
> produced heroes and heroines to meet the challenge ...[10]

The (not untypical) cluster of ideas contained in this flyposter from
the Newbury Bypass protest are worth investigating: the value ascribed
to natural 'heritage', history and 'the land'; the importance - to
England - of saving the countryside; the evocation of myth and mysticism in relation to Englishness; the un-interrogated assumptions
behind the 'our' of 'our heritage'. It's also worth noting the rather arch,
semi-parodic tone of the text (the original is in a quasi-medieval script).

The defence of, or the call for action on *behalf of*, (Mother) nature,
has been an important element of NVDA anti-road/runway protest.
Much cultural meaning is invested in the apparently self-evident (and
self-evidently 'good') category of nature or the natural, however.
'Nature' is viewed as an important locus of those values - integrity,
authenticity, directness - which, as we have seen, are now routinely
opposed to 'the political'. Since Romanticism enshrined nature 'as the
real world beyond the artificial world of society and politics' (Eder
p128), sacralised nature and the natural have continued to connote and
guarantee the authentic, the true, the real, that which is outside of and
untainted by (modern) culture. Anthony Giddens suggests an intimate
connection between 'nature' and 'tradition' - the latter he defines as
being based on ideas of 'ritual or revealed truth'(also important to the
countercultural relationship with nature) - and declares that we are
now living in a simultaneously post-traditional and post-natural
world.[11] While the latter is somewhat nonsensical - 'nature' is a discur-
sively constructed category: a pristine, pre-social, pre-discursive
'nature' is a fallacy, albeit a popular one, especially in the context under
discussion - I think Giddens is right in highlighting the slippage
between the terms 'nature' and 'tradition'. Such slippage allows things
that are unarguably cultural (e.g. ancient burial mounds, stone circles,

hedgerows) to become 'natural', a natural element of the natural landscape, or of an area of outstanding natural beauty - as long as they are 'ancient', loosely defined. 'Nature' meets 'Tradition', then, in the notion of the countryside.

What could be problematic about 'saving the countryside'? It seems self-evidently a good, politically neutral, thing to do. However, the idea(l) of the (imperilled) 'English countryside' is freighted with cultural meanings. 'Country' and 'land' of course have a double meaning: the natural/traditional landscape but also the nation. The countryside (specifically the southern English countryside) has, for at least a century, figured as the guarantor of a deep ethnic belonging and fundamental truths about the nation: the place where the 'real' England, and by implication the real English, are to be found. This has been a recurring, regressive trope in times of perceived crisis around the notion of England and Englishness. The rural idyll came to figure as the idea of 'home' which underpinned the British Imperial project. As the Empire, with its codes of robust manliness and racial superiority, came under stress, particularly during the reversals of the Boer war, a re-discovery of the countryside became central to discourses around a concern with the reinvigoration of the national racial 'stock' perceived to have been corrupted or gone soft in the cities. Through the two world wars to John Major's notorious 1993 'warm beer' evocation aimed at placating his Europhobic colleagues, Stanley Baldwin's famous dictum 'England is the country, and the country is England' has regrettably retained its currency.[12] The anti-modern, anti-urban veneration of 'our' threatened countryside is not, therefore, merely a neutral, quaint or (that peculiarly English characteristic) eccentric impulse, but has historically been central to the conception of Englishness and, at times, has been bound up with an insidious discourse of ethnic purity. The mystical sense of belonging evoked in anti-road protests tapping into national myths around 'the land' ought at least to be problematised, on the basis that such a mixture of nation and the land, particularly in conjunction with romanticism and ecologism, has historically been mobilised in a racist, 'volk-ish', anti-'cosmopolitan' discourse.[13]

The evocation of 'the land', the 'true spirit of England' emerging 'in times of great need' in the Newbury flier perhaps unconsciously, but certainly uncritically, draws on this 'traditional' equation of 'the land' and Englishness. This is not to say that the Newbury or Twyford anti-roads protestors or land rights campaigners ever propounded ethnic exclusivity. It would be wrong to interpret the fact that NVDA/DiY activism is overwhelmingly made up of young white people as a consequence of active exclusion. It is, however, possible that the 'unlikely alliances' with middle England and the rural squirearchy in which these two protests found themselves were eased by the uncritical way hegemonic ideas about an idealised English countryside were deployed. Such lack of awareness is the downside of the energising anti-theoretical, gestural nature of the DiY/NVDA critique.

We can think of this somewhat surprising, and surprisingly passionate, concern with England among young people - which emerged around the same time as the resolutely white monocultural idea of 'Britpop' and as Tony Blair's rather vapid 'New Britain' vision of a 'young country' - as a complex and misguided response to unsettling forces of globalisation and cultural fragmentation, a new crisis in the idea of nation. Clearly, a longing to belong, a comforting sense of authentic rootedness, is a desire which shouldn't be dismissed. But, at a time when a positive Englishness (*and* Britishness) badly needs re-imagining (modernising, even) this kind of backward-looking, ethnocentric merrie England discourse is at best counterproductive.

Further into the mystic

I find it difficult to get over my prejudice against the general mystic-holistic rhetoric in which the defense of nature in anti-road protests has often been couched, and with which the wider DiY Culture is involved.[14] Irrationalism is an affront to accepted notions of the political subject. It makes attempts at theoretical, and especially *political*, discussion like this one difficult.[15] But a defining feature of the 'life politics' of a cultural movement like DiY culture, and what disturbs orthodoxies concerning the political, is precisely the fact that the artificial separation of political action from other aspects of subjectivity - such as mystical beliefs - is no longer tenable.

We therefore need to take seriously DiY culture's espousal of mysticism and paganism 'the re-invention of ancient rituals and interest in 'magick' rather than adopt a 'dismissive rationalist contempt' or conveniently ignore it.[16] The problem is how to approach positively something that is an intrinsic feature of the discourse of the new activism. What are we to make, for example, of the animism which runs through anti-roads protest discourse - the feeling that the protestors, working *with* nature, can summon up a sort of protective occult force?[17]

Among other things, the language of mysticism is a way of talking about intense feelings of collective potential. Notions of mystical communion - and there is probably a connection here with the quasi-spiritualism of the ecstasy/dance culture experience - might be understood as a way of re-enchanting detraditionalised everyday life, as a characteristically postmodern nostalgia for 'depth' and something to believe in. It expresses aspects of social desire not catered for in our individualised culture of consumption or allowed by politics as it has been practised.[18] Mysticism generally stresses the experiential and privileges revealed 'wisdom', and as such is a corollary of DiY culture's general resistance to rational/intellectual/theoretical knowledge. As a way of making sense of contemporary reality, the investment of the world (usually the 'natural' world) with mystical, esoteric immanent meanings is, I would suggest, another instance of DiY culture's tendency to reject political analysis.

It must also be said that DiY/NVDA is a pretty druggy culture and the influence of psychoactive drugs shouldn't be minimised or ignored. Amid the moral panics, the consequences for the world-view of young people of widespread (and, since the 70s, democratised) use of drugs do not seem to have been considered. Drugs - particularly dope and acid - are not only about out and out hedonism; some use them in a more serious, exploratory - even spiritual - way. I'm not talking about a brain-damaged 'chemical generation' and neither am I arguing that there has been a total generational paradigm shift. I would simply suggest that everyday drug use in these contexts might produce, perhaps unqualifiable and unquantifiable, shifts in self- and world-perception.

Of course, getting into the mystical or spiritual doesn't always, or necessarily, involve the construction of a coherent cosmology or the full-blown commitment to a mystical belief system; the numbers who call themselves pagans or druids are minute. Furthermore, there is clearly a carnivalesque, playful aspect to the re-invention of pagan festivals and the 'primitive' styles and 'tribal' motifs - North American Indian drumming, Aboriginal didgeridoos, Celtic symbolism - widely adopted in the protest culture, just as, amongst its other meanings, there is a parodic aspect to the Newbury flyposter discussed above. I sense, however, that some sort of vague belief in things like 'vibes' or 'energies' or 'connections beneath the surface of things' is now commonplace among young people.[19] The enormous enthusiasm for the Glastonbury festival with all its 'new age-y' trappings might, for example, lend weight to my assertion.

Engaging with the urban

The fetishisation of the countryside in contemporary English culture is such that 'to display a lack of affection for the countryside, to confess to preferring city life, is regarded as perverse'.[20] I might already have made it obvious that I'm one of the perverse.

One way of internally differentiating DiY culture might be between those protests I've characterised as being mobilised in defence of Mother Earth/the English countryside, and those which engage with more complex, urban issues. I'm thinking, among others, of the protests against the M11 at 'Wanstonia', 'Reclaim the Streets' actions, 'Critical Mass' cyclists' traffic disruptions, the Wandsworth 'Pure Genius' land occupation, the Luton-based Exodus Collective's concern with providing homes and community facilities; campaigns which are anti- 'car culture' but also *for* community involvement in planning, housing, urban transport policy and so on. Given that most of us live in cities (might even continue to want to do so) and given that I doubt that our relationship with 'nature' is now *the* key political issue, it is these campaigns which, for me, are grappling with the more vital issues. They *engage* with modernity rather than adopting a 'fugitive' stance which would wish modernity away in the hope of a return to a 'simple', 'natural' or 'traditional' life.

With the weakening of affective class-based ties and the regrettable disintegration of the institutions of collectivism, there has been an increasing privatisation and atomisation of everyday life. What DiY activists call 'car-culture' is one symptom of this. Another is the wide-spread fear and loathing of cities in contemporary culture. The last two governments' response to urban problems has been to cast them in terms of 'crime' and 'anti-social behaviour' rather than to confront issues of public space, housing, transport. Policies have taken the form of an authoritarian and regulatory war on drugs, noisy neighbours, squeegee merchants, 'beggars', and children out after dark. The pene-tration of CCTV and private security into increasingly privatised civic spaces, for example, has gone unopposed by either of the two main parties. At the same time we have been treated to a tide of rhetoric about the need to re-establish the idea of community. 'Community' is a characteristically de-politicised notion, but even so I am not sure how its revival could be possible in cities in which the use of space is deter-mined by developers, which are choked with traffic and regulated in the interest of that ambiguous notion, 'security'. Campaigns which challenge the uses of urban space (the Wandsworth 'Pure Genius' land occupation was amongst other things about the way planning law works against the creative, community-based, human-needs use of often derelict city space; Reclaim the Streets (RTS) is about making streets pleasant and communal places to *be in*, rather than efficient or scary conduits to rush along) have done so by actually creating spaces to show what is possible. They have raised such issues by creating, however temporarily, imaginative public spaces; physical spaces and open, discursive spaces in which meanings can be made without predetermined agendas. And in so doing they have mounted an important critique of those processes of individualisation, privatisation and regulation which have made cities depressing places to live.

When Reclaim the Streets - which, for an afternoon, was a 'campaign group' of thousands of people - took over the M41 in west London (in a breathtaking feat of organisation) it/they/we created a space in which it seemed that anything could happen. This wasn't a 'festival' or a 'rave' in the organised, policed and commodified sense - although the sound systems provided an optional focus to the event - nor was it an orthodox 'protest march'. There was no platform, no speeches, no leaders, no formalised statement of demands. The RTS action created something like what the self-styled ontological anarchist' Hakim Bey calls a 'Temporary Autonomous Zone', a window onto creative possibility.[21] RTS's anonymous pamphleteers have made connections (and in an almost 'theoretical' register) beyond the simple anti-'car culture' issue - 'The streets are as full of capitalism as of cars and the pollution of capitalism is much more insidious' - while also insisting on the political nature of the carnival, and the importance of a pluralist, open city.

Political debate, like an active sense of community, requires public spaces, channels of communication. The fragmentation of forms of collectivism - a direct consequence of New Right policies of centralisation, privatisation, the attack on unions, the creation of the 'flexible' workforce - means that efforts like Reclaim the Streets can produce only a contingent and temporary collectivism, even though people take away an inspiration and a sense of possibility which outlasts the moment (Hakim Bey, incidentally, does not see 'temporary' in a negative sense, but understands it as dynamic, shape-shifting). The problem with any attempt to build wider alliances beyond DiY/NVDA protest is precisely the seemingly irreversible loss of any form of collectivist political culture. There are obvious, positive things to be said for detraditionalisation: a weakening of deference and of proscribed gender roles are both, for example, part of the process. But the danger is that we are left with an unbridgeable physical/institutional/cultural gap between ways of doing politics with different (maybe incommensurate) visions and aims, with little in the way of a common arena - a public sphere - in which they can talk.

Down the road

We can't, then, talk about DiY culture/NVDA in terms of a coherent politics based on some objective class community of interest, around either distributive justice, or (despite what Klaus Eder might suggest) a changed orientation towards 'nature'. And there are other reasons to be pessimistic about future alliance-building and growth. It needs to be acknowledged that many of those involved in DiY culture actively enjoy their underground, anti-authority status. There is a degree of self-conscious rebelliousness in these protests which works against the potential for forming wider alliances with the 'straight world' of progressive/left politics. In the sense that DiY culture has been formed by its marginalisation in the unfriendly circumstances it grew up in, it is understandably resistant to assimilation. I think a certain symbiosis has existed between DiY culture's romantic outsider stance, and the dominant political culture's urge for middle-of-the-road consensus. Furthermore, it seems doubtful that new Labour's inclusive society: family oriented, stakeholding and responsible, a somewhat conformist christian liberal utopia, could include space for DiY culture's weirdos. As is the case with Communitarianism, which has influenced new Labour's thinking, this 'inclusive society' rather than being dynamically, democratically in process, seems to presuppose an already existing conflict-free consensus which need only be 'revealed'.[22] It seems some groups must necessarily be excluded under the sign of the 'anti-social'. Similarly, for reasons already touched on, DiY culture has, to say the least, an ambivalent attitude towards the 'official' media. While many of the protests seem designed to be as outrageously spectacular as possible, activists often seem resistant to, or resentful of, the media-isation of 'their' politics. The current problem, given that only that which happens in the media seems to constitute 'politics', is that avoiding serious engagement with orthodox media channels facilitates the depoliticisation and decontextualisation of their protest. It becomes a protest in a vacuum and doesn't really disturb the structures of power. Unless political power is radically decentralised DiY culture and representative politics may either simply remain indifferent to each other, or we will see more of the same authoritarian, pathologising response to this emergence of collective protest based on new, contingent solidarities.

What I've tried to suggest here is another way of looking at DiY culture. One that perhaps reads it less positively - in a less celebratory fashion - than has generally been the case, but in a way which provides a focus for thinking about what we mean by (radical) politics. DiY culture's post-industrial, non-class-based collectivism is positive and its affective and mystical aspects point up the bankruptcy of narrowly 'rational' conceptions of politics and the political subject. At the same time, I find the utopian 'back to the land' aspects of this contradictory protest culture somewhat wilfully simplistic and essentially un-radical, and the resistance to 'politics' and theory reflective of wider and depressing cultural trends. I wouldn't suggest that NVDA anti-roads protests, for example, are a soft option, or that they haven't been valuable in highlighting transport policy as an important instance of free-market madness, and incidentally revealing just how deeply attacks on civil liberties have run. They strike me as both romantic in Klaus Eder's 'bourgeois fugitive' sense, *and also* as an important critique of hegemonic rationalist modernism. It's easy to understand, and to feel, the attraction of abstractions like 'simplicity' or 'nature', and presumably most people can support environmental concerns (if not necessarily of an orthodox conservationist type). But the more pressing need is to find ways of engaging *politically* with modernity (science, industry and the global economy) which don't involve reverting to a new medievalism. We need to find ways of living together and of belonging (and of 'being English') which are not based on 'tradition' or ethnocentric notions of pastoral arcadia, and ways of doing politics which challenge what we currently mean by the political but don't abandon *thinking* politically.

Notes

1. The best example I have come across is *Squall* magazine: PO Box. 8959 London N19 5HW. Any issue will include details of the current campaigns.
2. *Guardian*, 24 May 1997.

3. Timothy Bewes, *Cynicism and Postmodernity*, Verso, London 1997.
4. Roy Hattersley castigates new Labour in roughly the same terms 'Pragmatism must not still conscience', *Guardian*, 14 May 1997.
5. Bewes *op. cit.* p27.
6. Flyposters for this event can still be seen around London. The juxtaposition of the slogan: 'Never Mind the Ballots ... Reclaim the Streets!' a still from Charlie Chaplin's satire on industrial mass production 'Modern Times' is, I think, interesting in the light of my arguments here.
7. See George MacKay *Senseless Acts of Beauty*, London, Verso 1996. *Guardian* columnist and The Land is Ours campaigner George Monbiot has been keen on the history of 'enclosure', Hill's *The World Turned Upside Down*, Penguin, London 1991.
8. Klaus Eder, *The New Politics of Class: Social Movements and Cultural Dynamics in Advanced Societies*, Sage, London 1993.
9. Part of what Ulrich Beck calls our 'Risk Society' or Anthony Giddens the condition of 'manufactured uncertainty' see Beck, *Risk Society*, Sage, London 1992, and Giddens, *Beyond Left and Right*, Polity Press, Cambridge 1994.
10. Quoted in an interesting and involving first-person account of the Newbury protest: Merrick, *Battle for the Trees*, Godhaven Inc., Leeds 1996 (common era), p3.
11. Giddens, *op. cit.* p46.
12. Examples abound: the commentator on TV coverage of the journey of Diana, Princess of Wales' body to its final resting place was prompted to refer to a shot of the Northamptonshire countryside as a 'pure piece of England', a description that would have been unthinkable for earlier shots of the hearse's progress through north London.
13. Patrick Wright has written extensively on unsavoury, fascistic manifestations of the connection between 'blood and soil' in his *On Living in an Old Country*, Verso, London 1985; and *The Village that Died for England*, Jonathan Cape, London 1995.
14. My antipathy is based on a feeling that mysticism/holism - or new ageism- is often politically reactionary in character. New ageism too often reproduces, in its emphasis on 'self-actualisation', its stress on the individual's responsibility for attaining individual 'goals', the 'if-you-want-it-badly-enough-you-can-get-it' rethoric of the Thatcherite self-made man or woman.
15. I'm writing this in the days following the death of Diana, Princess of Wales, when political and cultural commentators have had a real struggle dealing with the (irrational?) tides of emotion apparently gripping the nation.

16. Mike Waite, 'To Stanworth and Beyond: Reflections on DiY politics and the Anti-Roads Movement' in *Soundings*, Issue 3, Summer 1996. The same rationalist contempt might dismiss as trivial protests for the 'freedom to party'.

17. Indeed, a 1989 Gallup poll apparently found that 72 per cent of British people 'have an awareness of a sacred presence in nature'. Quoted in Paul Heelas, *The New Age Movement*, Blackwell, Oxford 1996, p109.

18. See Wendy Wheeler, 'Nostalgia isn't Nasty: The Postmodernising of Parliamentary Democracy' in Mark Perryman (ed), *Altered States: Postmodernism, Politics, Culture*, Lawrence & Wishart, London 1994, for a good discussion of the way contemporary political practice disallows aspects of social desire and circumscribe 'the political subject'.

19. Heelas *op. cit.* p33.

20. Jan Marsh, *Back to the Land: the Pastoral Impulse in Victorian England from 1880 to 1914*, Quartet, London 1982, p246.

21. *T.A.Z. The Temporary Astronomous Zone, Ontological Anarchy, Poetic Terrorism*, Autonomedia, New York 1991.

22. Bewes, *op. cit.*, p86.

Hijabs in our midst

Noshin Ahmad

The issue of Islam and women is a contentious and controversial one within academia, the media and Muslim cultures themselves. Discourses on Islam and gender tend to focus on the subjugation of women by Muslim men. This then comes to be read as our faith. Issues such as cliterodectomy, wife battering and cloistering are seen as symbols of barbaric Islamic traditions when, in fact, they are prohibited in Islam. I do not wish to apologise for or exonerate Islam; what I do want to highlight is the sometimes huge gaps between the sanctioned practices of Islam and the actual behaviour of Muslims. Women who do embrace the religion have not succumbed to the irrational, but are engaging with Islam in various ways. The veil/hijab is the most visible signifier of the differentness of Islamic culture, and this will be my focus.

Here's a little anecdote, the subject of which I have to deal with frequently. One day as I was walking to the tube station from my university, I bumped into a postgrad classmate and we got chatting. Well into the conversation she said to me 'You're a walking contradiction Noshin, you don't strike me as a person who would wear a hijab. You're educated, opinionated, independent, and assertive, so why do you wear it? When I see these little Muslim women on the trains bundled up in their scarves, I feel so sorry for them. They look so ... *oppressed!*' We finished off the sentence in unison. When I told her it was solely out of choice, and that my parents had neither forced or even asked me to do it, she was incredulous. She could not fathom the thought that any woman would want to cover her hair out of her own free will, implying that only ignorant and passive women would wear the veil.

In Britain and the West, representations of Islam focus on its supposed discouragement, if not denial, of women's right to an education, work, financial independence, political activism, choice of marriage partner and geographical mobility – basically the intellectual capability and space to pursue their own goals and to have their own ambitions. These representations ignore the fact that Prophet Mohammed's first and much loved wife Khadija was a successful businesswoman for whom he worked before and during their marriage. Furthermore, in the Qur'an it states that it is the duty of every person – male and female – to acquire knowledge and educate themselves. It is precisely these factors and the openness of Islam to women that has attracted them.

Representations of women who accept Islam have pejorative connotations. Women are shown to be helplessly subjugated by mad mullahs and male family members, burdened by their veils, backward, and passive. They are regarded as traitors to their sex, having internalised patriarchal ideologies of their inferior status. I do not wish to repeat the common and sometimes over simplified grief about the media conspiracy against Islam, but I think it is worthwhile to emphasise the dangerous effects of media representations.

Islam is often presented as a threat to the dominant host culture – Islam is irrational, medieval, encroaching and engulfing – and Muslims are compartmentalised into rigid stereotypes. 'Islamic Fundamentalism' has come to *mean* Islam: some fanatical members of Islamist groups are held as spokesmen for the entire Muslim diaspora. In a Baudrillardian sense the media has created a caricature of the image, which then becomes a simulation so that the image becomes 'more real than the real'. Conceptualising Islam/Muslims and other groups in rigid stereotypes results in the racialisation of religion. Minority communities are not only perceived as internally unified, homogeneous entities with no class and gender differences, but also as *defined* by religion, e.g. Islam.

Globalisation and the postmodern development of local narratives has created an indefinite number of histories and forms of knowledge which theoretically should be non-hierarchical and relative to one another. Despite postmodernism's alleged sensitivity to multiculturalism there has not been a substantial effort to meet Islam halfway. Cross-cultural mobility which has led to the increase of veiled women in the public spaces of Britain, has not resulted in the development of a pluralist concept of the veil. It is still regarded as primitive and a symbol of Islamic militancy and 'fundamentalism'.

Younger 'British' Muslims, the children of first and second generation immigrants who were born and brought up amidst 'British' social values, are represented as rebelling against this imagined 'fundamentalism'. Time and again the problem of forced marriage surfaces and girls are reported as having been duped to vacation in their parents' country of origin, unaware that soon they will be married off for a huge dowry. Another popular narrative is of Muslim girls running away with non-Muslim boyfriends because of family pressure to marry them off in a loveless match. Here the family are sent to trace their steps, kidnap the girl, and beat the crap out of the boyfriend. Tragic stories such as Jean Sassoon's *Princess*, and that of the two British-Yemeni women who had been sold into wedded slavery are shocking. While no one doubts that these events occasionally take place and that their impact on the individuals involved is profound, the way in which incidents are represented denigrates women's relationship to Islam.

There is rarely an attempt to contextualise media representations within an Islamic framework based on the Qur'an and Sunnah (the traditions and practices of Prophet Mohammad). Consequently, Islam comes to be judged by the actions of Muslims, rather than the judging of Muslims by Islam. Docility and the unquestioning submission to male relatives is often understood as the role of females within the Muslim family. The fact that in Islam a marriage is a contract between two mutually consenting partners, in which a dowry (mehr) is paid to the bride (rather than vice versa, or to her parents), and in which divorce can be initiated by both partners, is overlooked. Prophet Mohammad even said 'The best among you are those kindest to their wives'.

It is misleading to take cultural, political and social, patriarchal practices of Muslim men and define these as 'Islamic'. In many cases the oppression of women is not a religious condition, but a political issue, because their rights and interests conflict with male advantages. Perhaps part of the problem is that the examination of Muslim people's lives overstates its explanatory power. Gender inequality is therefore mistakenly blamed on the influence of Islam over the lives of individuals. The premise is that once Islam is removed from the equation, equality will follow. Less attention is paid to the worldwide problem that women have very little access to matriarchal interpretations and spiritual teachings of Islam. The eminent female jurists, scholars, philosophers and activists of Prophet Mohammad's time, along with their causes and actions, have long been written out of history.

Although marginal at present the interest in recuperating and rewriting this history is slowly but surely being taken up by Muslim feminists. Many Muslim women are unaware of the rights Islam has afforded them; those who are aware are made to feel that they have to defend their 'privileges'. Such women argue that even in non-Muslim communities gender inequality is still a reality. Further, conventional pronouncements on Islam fail to distinguish between ideal Islamic behaviour and the norms of their communities. For example, in my experience people have often asked me about my parent's attitude to female education – they tend to think of my parents as liberated because they have always encouraged me in my studies. This question is asked because people judge Islam by the behaviour of Muslim men who may prohibit education, among their daughters and come to hold the stereotypical view that it is forbidden in Islam.

There are different ways of wearing the hijab. The most common form is wearing a scarf or khimar (length of cloth) to cover one's hair, leaving the face exposed. The covering of the face is not necessary, it is up to personal choice as it should be in all Muslim societies. No matter what one wears – dresses, skirts, shalwaar kameez, sarees – the main object is that the flesh and curves of the body should not be apparent. Many women wear a jalbaab, a loose tunic, or an abaya, a long black cloak, over their clothes but under these they are as 'normal' and lively as ever, donning 'typically' Western clothes: jeans, T-shirts of their favourite bands, jewellery, with trendy haircuts. In Britain more and more women are taking up the hijab, nor are these girls and women 'brainwashed' into doing so. Many are in fact educated, opinionated, independent, and assertive.

How and in what context the veil is worn, in Britain, Algeria, or Saudi Arabia, means different things. Unfortunately, deproblematising the polyvalency of the veil, inevitably leads to its homogenisation and how it figures in Muslim women's lives. That is, their lives are made simple, its complexities hidden under symbols which stand in its place, all veiled women are lumped together with the implication that they all wear the veil for the same reasons. The fact that they live in different countries under different political, class and social situations is disregarded. If a woman wears the hijab that is the first and foremost aspect about her which is noticed, she is 'over determined', judged irrespective of who and what she is. There is little attempt to move beyond or understand the piece of cloth and the woman behind it.

In this way the veil is a symbol of otherness. It is conceived either as a symbol of Islamic extremism, or it is romanticised within an orientalist tradition. In the latter case the veil shrouds a beautiful, exotic, and carnal woman who frustrates the voyeur. The veiled woman becomes presence and absence simultaneously – especially if her face and clothing are hidden from gaze. She is represented as being out of reach and possession; beyond control. These representations are limiting, they do not acknowledge women's self realisations, their competence, or their agency, autonomy and power. Less attention is given to the personal meaning of the hijab as an obligatory form of dress and/ or a chosen way of clothing. There is no explaining or questioning as to why many Muslim women want to wear the veil, instead we are bombarded with paternalistic explanations which argue the reasons why women should not wear it and why it is a form of gender oppression.

Muslim women use the veil as a way of making a statement about their social position, identity and personal politics, and these statements differ from person to person. Some women stress the liberating potential of veiling and the strategic benefits of public anonymity. For others it is a question of maintaining modesty and respectability. The wearing of the veil has both a symbolic and practical dimension. Some Muslim women view dominant Western conventions of femininity as turning women's beauty into a product of capitalism to be bought and sold, encouraging women to consume fast obsolete fashions. Wearing the veil makes a statement of non-conformity. Communicating with the outside world, without being on show, is also a way of not conforming. Women have taken up the hijab for many reasons such as keeping their appearance private, demarcating boundaries and public space, and feeling secure and protected from sexual harassment and lecherous stares. In Britain it is also used to acknowledge and reassert cultural backgrounds and family roots. Pride in being a Muslim is also cited as one of the reasons women have taken up the hijab/veil.

But in the dominant media representations the veil *becomes* the practising Muslim woman. The specific historical conditions under which women, politics, Islam and power interact are ignored . The veil generally symbolises feminine identity in Islam, in contrast to the way it is sometimes used as a form of oppression within certain Muslim cultures. This conceptualisation of the veil can be dehumanising, Muslim woman's identity is lost, she remains 'blinkered'. Only if the

Muslim woman throws off her scarf will she be free to express herself fully.

People have often asked me if I sleep with it on, do I wear it when I change my clothes, and is it on when I am having sex? It is basically regarded as an article of clothing that cramps, constrains, and constricts, and which symbolises women's invisibility and subordinate socio-political status in Islam. It renders them anonymous, unapproachable, and even abnormal. I know that I am often regarded with suspicion. It is almost as if at any time I shall go into a trance and start reciting Arabic gibberish, or that I'll knock you unconscious by bashing a Qur'an on your head and start preaching the evil of your ways (while you're out cold on the floor!). People tend to think that practising Muslims cannot come to grips with reality and that they sit and pray all day. However a fundamental part of Islam is the balance of deen and duniya – of religion and the world. On an occasion that I was wearing platform shoes and walking across a pedestrian crossing, a misplaced step saw me sink to my knees. An old woman coming the other way took one look at me, shook her head, and said 'Stop praying in the middle of the road'.

Living in Britain, Muslim women are straddling two worlds. We have to negotiate conflicting and competing cultural, social and political values. While postmodern globalisation has blurred the boundaries of cultural distinctiveness and authenticity, there has also been a resurgence in the commitment to traditional and religious practices. When second and third generation immigrants wear the veil with jeans, skirts and designer wear, it becomes a public sign of personal religious faith.

Dress and fashion have always been aesthetic mediums for expressing views on ideas, beliefs and desires. If we are living in a postmodern world with secularisation and the dislocation of the social and the political, then perhaps wearing the hijab is one manifestation of resolving how to live in our world of doubt. Akbar Ahmed argues that the postmodern rejection of established religion, coinciding with a powerful revival of Islam, is a paradox.[1] Faced with uncertainty and radical doubt, more and more young Muslims are turning to Islam for anchorage. Perhaps women are wearing the veil because it becomes the means by which the fragmented self can present itself as a whole. Wearing the hijab stabilises our individual identity and assuages the fragmented self by connecting us to our social group. Worn in different ways, it is an effective form of individual yet collective expression.

Emancipation from religious moralism and the rise of secularism in Europe is regarded as having led to greater freedom of self-expression and individuality. This has had huge significance for women's sexual liberation and ability to be in charge and in control of their bodies. Simultaneously many feminists regard wearing the veil as contradicting and working against their historical struggle for gender equality and independence. There is concern that the veil inhibits women from expressing their sexuality. But there is not only one way to express feminine sexuality. Veiled women's sexualities can be assertive or playful, boring or seductive, public or private – she too can inhabit multi-faceted subjectivities. The Muslim woman is aware, perceptive, and critically engages with the veil, her body, and her environment, as she sees fit. Women negotiate and use different strategies to lay claim to their bodies.

Some women find the topless page three girls aimed at titillating and firing male fantasies dehumanising. They object to the continual use of women as sex objects to further patriarchal advantages. Others, like the Spice Girls, take charge of their bodies by proclaiming the right to bare what they wish, when they wish and in front of whom they wish in the name of 'Girl Power'. I am not taking a stance against any of this, but what I do not understand is why the veil and covering one's body have to be divorced from feminist politics? I am not assuming that there is only one feminist position on the veil, but it appears that in the West wearing the veil and feminism are regarded as mutually exclusive. Why does the veil go against White European (Liberal) Feminism's struggle for self-determination? I am not arguing that within all cultural and historical conditions the veil has had liberating affects. On the contrary, forcefully inflicting the veil has been, and still is, an expression of the ownership of women in many societies. What I am arguing is that we need to examine the cultural relativity of the veil without simply dismissing it as oppressive, especially since it is becoming more prevalent.

I would argue it is erroneous to regard the resurgence of hijab as an imposed constraint on women's freedom of movement and self-actualisation. In my experience many women wearing the hijab are young and educated, mostly university students. They are wearing it in the context of a British society which does not expect them to do so, so it is not out of social pressure or obligation. As for family pressure, those that wish not to wear it take it off as soon as they leave the boundary of home. Taking the hijab and veil is an active and deliberate choice that

Muslim women in this society make. Often this choice clashes with their own family and cultural background. When an old family friend came to dinner, the first thing she said when she saw my sister and me in hijab was 'Isn't that a bit much?'

This is illustrative of the generation gap emerging between (in my experience, South Asian) Muslim immigrants and their British-born children. A gap not always marked by the younger's attachment to Western secular ideals, but by the rejection of non-Islamic cultural practices of Muslims and the growing adherence to sanctioned practices of Islam. Events such as the 'Rushdie affair', the plight of the Bosnians, and the Gulf War are much quoted examples that have prompted young Muslims to question their identity, and in the process to strengthen their affiliations with Islam. Contrary to popular belief, this is not a simple rejection of the West, nor does it always result in a turn to 'extremism', or as it is widely termed 'fundamentalism'.

Many Muslims object to this highly charged term, questioning who has defined it, and the nature of its definition. In Islam there are basic principles you have to practice and believe in: that there is only one God and that Prophet Mohammed was his last messenger (in a long succession including Adam, Abraham, Ishmael, Moses, Lot, Noah and Jesus – all of whom Muslims believe in). It is obligatory to fast in the month of Ramadhan, to give yearly alms to the poor, and to make a pilgrimage to Mecca if it can be afforded financially and physically. These are the fundamentals of Islam – if you do not believe in them then you are not a Muslim. Violent extremism is a totally different issue. Despite media portrayals not all Muslims are out to kill Jews, homosexuals, Salman Rushdie (!) and basically all those who do not convert to our ways.

Being a Muslim and living in Britain are not incompatible. Many young British Muslims express strong affiliations with both Britain and Islam. They 'mix n' match' aspects from both cultures to create an identity that works for them. This hybrid position could be promising once Muslims have stopped being regarded as the other. By wearing the veil I am not rejecting British culture, neither am I trying to authenticate my position as simply 'Muslim'. For me these two things are intricately linked. If I try to draw circles around one or the other, it is easy to create dangerous differences and ghettoise both cultures. So if I want to have roast beef and Yorkshire pudding, I want it to be halal roast beef!

Note

1. Akbar S. Ahmed, *Postmodernism and Islam: Predicament and Promise*, Routledge, London 1996, p27.

Paradigm lost? Youth and pop

Rupa Huq

Rock, initially at any rate, was a contemporary incitement to mindless
fucking and arbitrary vandalism: screw and smash music.

George Melly, 'Revolt into Style', 1970

Within everyone of my generation there's an aspiring rock musician
waiting to get out.

Tony Blair, *Daily Telegraph*, 27/7/97

What is the meaning of pop in the approach to the millennium? With
Oasis photographed with Tony Blair over drinks at No. 10 – echoing
Harold Wilson's MBE awards for the Beatles – are the 1990s just the
1960s upside down? Pop does not exist as a hermetically sealed category; text and context are indivisible. Questions of society, politics and
economics feed into its cause and effect relationship with changing
times.

Pop music has historically been pivotal to western post war youth
culture. Rock and roll is privileged in youth culture's unholy trinity
alongside sex and drugs. Revolving around the poles of idealism and
hedonism, pop marries cathartic youthful self-expression, empower-
ment and liberation from parental norms, with a parallel pleasure ethic.
Ross and Rose (1994) list pop's functions as: 'a daily companion, social
bible, commercial guide and spiritual source'. Music also offers
escapism. As Chambers (1986) claims, youth culture offers 'a chance to
escape your time, your circumstances, your history.' The pop-youth
paradigm is now well established. The Who's affirmation of it: 'Hope I
die before I get old' was later echoed by the Jesus and Mary Chain in

word ('I wanna die like JFK/ I wanna die on a sunny day/ I wanna die like Jesus Christ/ I wanna die on a bed of spikes') and Kurt Cobain indeed, via his suicide note proclamation 'It's better to burn out than fade away'. However a number of developments in the 1990s seemed to suggest that pop's assured place at youth culture's core was more precariously located than ever before. It had become time to think the unthinkable: that pop music is no longer youth music (Redhead, 1989:8).

After four decades – now the subject of numerous commentaries, books and even university degrees – pop has proved to be durable and influential in contemporary society. However its ubiquitousness can be seen to undermine its usefulness. In an ironic reversal, forty years of pop history means that it is steeped in the past. In January 1985 the youth magazine, *Jamming*, featured Simon Frith, originator of 'the sociology of rock' via his book of the same name, as something of an eccentric oddity given his age, academic position and love of pop. 'What is a 38 year old senior lecturer in sociology doing writing about rock music?', the piece demanded. Frith replied: 'I feel that I'm a 38 year old who listens to music and changes my tastes with much more rapidity and has more open ears than most'. His position now seems odd because, in the current climate, the thirtysomethings dominate pop criticism and fandom. In 1995 Frith commented: 'Age is a funny thing in music. For young people now rock and roll is old peoples' music'.[1]

In a variation of the slacker/Generation X argument, apocalyptic visions of the imminent implosion of pop music appeared in the early 1990s, in both popular and academic discourse – fittingly – given the cross-over between the two. Factors advanced as nails in pop's coffin included the threat of cyberspace, radio stations based on nostalgia programming, Australian soap opera, revivalism, cover bands and re-releases. Within academia, Paglia (1992) argued that rock/pop had moved too far from the margins to the centre, swallowed up by dominant culture in the process: 'Rock is a victim of its own success. What once signified rebellion is now a high school affectation. White suburban youth, rock's main audience, is trapped in creature comforts. Everything comes to them secondhand, through TV. And they no longer have direct contact with folk music, blues, the oral repositiories of love, hate, suffering and redemption'. From popular quarters former punk music scribe turned cultural critic Tony Parsons announced the 'death of pop'. (*The Times* 21/11/92)

Signs that pop was fast metamorphosing from its original remit into a market-driven concern seemed to be confirmed by David Bowie's transformation into a Wall Street investment floated on the stock market.[2] Similarly when George Michael confessed 'I think you might be a little shocked' in the High Court in September 1993 he was not referring to 'lock up your daughter' rock and roll decadence, but to the multi-million figure of how much he was worth. The Mercury Music Prize and Brit awards also seem to illustrate the extent of pop's passage from anti- to arch-establishment, with big prize money, commercial sponsors and pop reduced to a competitive sport. The ascendance of the 'serious' rock-press for the more discerning, ie, older reader is also significant here. Following the success of Q magazine, conceived for the reader who had outgrown teen pop mag *Smash Hits*, EMAP magazines launched the title *Mojo* for grown-up Q fans in 1994. The emphasis was placed on reviews and retrospective features and career profiles with assessments of stereo equipment signalling a shift to the dream of aspiration and 'lifestyle journalism'.

The 1990s saw the second coming of a number of pop acts, relaunched from beyond the grave to a young, although far from unsuspecting, audience. Rob Partridge took over the management of Jimi Hendrix and the Doors in 1991, turning around their respective careers from discarded back-catalogue acts to chart sellers via repackaged greatest hits compilations. In 1994 he told me 'It's great. They don't answer back, they're never hung over, they're never late'.[3] In this way pop, rather than existing as an ongoing entity, is packaged as a complete body of work, like opera or classical composers. The record companies are the gatekeepers with the defining role of deciding what is worthy of being 'classic'. The publication of weighty encyclopaedic tomes concerning rock (Hardy and Laing 1995, Savage and Kureishi 1995) complements the process. By 1997 an unprecedented six Oasis tribute groups co-existed with the genuine article. In 1993 and 1995 the (living) members of the Velvet Underground and Sex Pistols further punctured their mystique by reforming to tour. The Pistols' John Lydon (née Rotten) told the world's assembled press that their motive was money. Within minutes of the band putting down their instruments after their Finsbury Park gig, already in the can was the recording. It was released weeks later for those who had been unfortunate enough not to attend.

Part of the problem with the 'pop is dead' argument is that it all too clearly reveals its propagators' own age-based prejudices, coloured by the generational expectations. A worthy subcultural successor to punk has been sought in vain by journalists and academics alike (Redhead, 1989, Bloomfield, McRobbie, 1993: 410). Parsons tellingly railed against the 1990s as 'an unthinkable betrayal to those of us in our thirties'. With pop's insurgent sting neutered as it is normalised from its rebel roots, pop is undeniably changing, but it is also taking on new meanings. If we take rock to be that music of guitar-based melodies of regular pace, perhaps a case can be advanced for rock rupture and the supplementing of the traditional rock formula by other entities: variations on a theme.

90s music: rave on

Umbillically connected to rave – itself with us since 1987's acid house moral panic – the function of dance music is self explanatory. Yet as Thornton (1995:71) identifies 'Dancing is still frequently stigmatized as being uncritical and mindless to the extent that it can debase the music with which it is associated', a point also made by Thomas (1993) and McRobbie (1984). Importantly there is no single unified 'rave culture', just as dance music is far from homogeneous. There is a huge divergence between upmarket superclubs such as Cream in Liverpool or London's Ministry of Sound, and the randomly occuring, entry *gratis*, ad hoc illegal affairs in deserted premises. The unlicensed rave, unlike the traditional rock concert, is non-linear. Place and time are not fixed, being at the mercy of police pressure. The raver dances like there is no tomorrow because tomorrow quite literally just ain't going to happen. Rave staple, techno music, is the ultimate 'be-there' joke: mood music rendered meaningless when divorced from its surroundings. Few would listen to nine hours of uninterrupted techno at home yet it makes perfect sense at a rave.

Other 'death of pop' allegations have been aimed at cultural forms which have displaced pop's force, but dance music is different, because all of its offspring – techno, hard house, handbag, ambient, hardcore, drum and bass, intelligent, Goa trance – are original music. However, its repeating hypnotic rhythms and forms, based on BPM (beats per minute) in place of human voice and melody (the lifeblood of traditional pop), can make for uneasy listening to the conventional ear. Dance music subverts such authenticity-laden norms with the computer sampler, through which the composer passes other people's music, to be reconstituted in postmodern sonic collage. As Beadle

(1993:138) writes: '...to a computer literate generation, this technology simplifies the concept of music-making'. Techno does not rely on regular music notation being recorded straight onto tape thus by-passing the need for additional musicians to play the other parts. As Langlois asserts (1992:231) 'musicianship' is in its most generally accepted sense is virtually non-existent'. The very term, techno, implies technical expertise over passion, emotion or soul. Claims that it is not music at all (eg 'Acid House: How Dare they Call It Music?' (*Sun* 7/10/88) are a variation of the high-low dichotomy that has haunted cultural studies since Adorno. The sonic abandon of 1990s dance has importantly been a liberation from the old certainties.

1990s dance music shares the demystification of the music element of punk: the 1970s DIY ideal of guitar, three chords and enthusiasm updated with a pile of records and the right mixing equipment. Punk's anti-star backlash against the muse culture of 1970s progressive rock is also taken to its extreme as the DJ, formerly the anoymous backroom boy, paradoxically becomes the star – preceded by reputation alone. The name Carl Cox or Fabio on a flyer is a magnet for audiences who wouldn't recognise their hero even if they fell over him in the bottled water queue. DJs do not talk throughout the 'performance', and their wares are often created on an ad-hoc basis to suit audience demands by mixing tracks, rendering no commercially available original. Mainstream releases usually follow from favourable impact on the dance floor rather than the reverse. Interestingly enough, this advanced musical form has succeeded in reviving the once considered moribund medium of vinyl. Langlois (1992:229) argues that that this shift of meaning makes the DJ's role as 'simultaneously ... performer, marketer and composer of the music'. Rave DJs are unlike the covential 'pop star' just as rave goers pride themselves on the lack of a traditional 'disco' – sexual cattle market atmosphere – thanks to 'the hug drug' Ecstasy having replaced alcohol as social lubricant of choice.

The internal aims of youth culture have always attached a high value to 'not selling out' just as its academic study through the prism of subculture has always insisted on 'authenticity'. Yet in a sense 'underground' is a euphemism for 'unpopular'; hence the audible cries of treachery accompanying any once-underground artist's attainment of commercial success or signing to a major label, seen as a loss of artistic 'purity' to market forces. Jungle music for example, existed in specialist clubs and on pirate radio, perhaps eighteen months before the charting of drum and bass darling Goldie. Underground labels are the alternative economy of the music business. The passage of jungle from underground to overground was marked with the sucessful reincarnation of indie miserablists, Everything But the Girl, as a drum and bass outfit in 1996. Essex boys, Prodigy, meanwhile have a foot in the pop camp while retaining their original techno sensibilities. Their phenomenal sucess in 1997 earned them the headline slot at the Glastonbury festival, Mecca of alternative rock, and a number one album in America – a feat that not even Oasis have been able to pull off. Their electrifying live performance with the two vocalists upfront is pure pop spectacle. Certainly dance music as a whole has had far-reaching effects. Rave's music can be heard literally everywhere, from supermarkets to television advertising. High street nightclubs host regular rave-nights in a controlled environment. No pop tune is complete without a DJ remix, aimed at a rave-hungry generation of consumers.

Rave practices also demonstrate a spatial shift away from the transatlantic 'American Dream', so prevalent in early youth culture writing (Hebdige, 1986). European leanings can be seen in Belgian newbeat and Frankfurt techno. Ecstasy is manufactured in Holland, where progressive measures on its testing at raves, to identify counterfeit lethal prohibition-style chemical concoctions, are often cited as the way forward by UK drug workers. The Love parade in Berlin is established as the leading world rave event and, lest we forget, British justice spawned the Criminal Justice Act to rein in rave. With the roots of rave contested (variously located in Chicago, UK Northern Soul clubs, the Balearic Islands and Goa) dance music's internationalist influences embrace various world musics. However, one should be wary of Goa tourism, whether played out on Indian beaches or UK dancefloors. It is admissible to the fairweather raver to spend the summer or weekend locked in an Ecstasy haze claiming that they are 'getting back to nature' in being 'primitive' and 'tribal', but this imposition of value systems is tantamount to cultural colonisation, invoking bogus notions of bohemia based on a simultaneous white fascination and fear towards blackness. This temporary and transient 'dropping out' is a conscious decision presuming the existence of a place to drop out from, one not open to citizens of the 3rd World. What the Sex Pistols called 'a cheap holiday in other people's misery'.

1990s dance music is fraught with paradoxes. Despite its technological bent, its thematics and imagery are often simplistic. The logo that came to symbolise the 'second summer of love', itself a deja-vu of an earlier moment in youth culture mythology, was the ecstatically happy smiley face. The closest that rave comes to the pseudo political posturing of youth culture sloganeering of yesteryear (cf punk's 'anarchy in the UK' and hippie's 'be reasonable, demand the impossible') is the distinctly un-idealistic 'rave on'. Nonetheless it was techno-culture that bit back when it was threatened by the Criminal Justice Bill, with a strong youth resistance campaign.

The term 'dance music' itself masks a myriad of musical sub-genres. To claim a dislike of 'dance music', as Morrissey did in the Smiths' track 'Panic' of 1986 with its key refrain 'Hang the DJ', is to take the same position as parents who make sweeping generalisations about all modern 'pop music' sounding the same. The 1990s dancefloor has a place for everyone. It makes more sense then to talk of 'dance musics' with varying characteristics. Hyper-rapid paced techno music is associated with ecstacy, a psychoactive drug (upper) for the frenetic pace of the dancefloor. Meanwhile the slow doodlings of ambient, described by Toop (1995) as 'the oxymoron of acid-house – dance music for sitting still', are consumed with cannabis, a psychotropic drug (downer) at the post rave chill-out. Jungle offers two discordant rthymic lines; slow loping bass and jittery breakbeats. Importantly, just as there is more to youth culture than just pop in the 1990s there is more to pop than just dance music.

Britpop (vs dance) – problematics, politics

Britpop provided an alternative soundtrack to the 1990s, stamped with zeitgeist and unremittingly retrogressive. Butressed by media revelry in an alleged renaissance of Quant era style Carnaby Street swinging London, for anyone old enough to remember – or care – Britpop spelled back to the future with the 1960s as the template.[4] Its musically unadventurous adherence to guitars was compensated by its cartoon character-like personalities, the very antithesis of faceless 1990s dance. The 'Who's the greatest?' phoney war between chief protagonists Manchester's Oasis and Colchester's Blur, recalled the Beatles vs Stones rivalry. It made *Newsnight* in summer 1995 and generated acres of column interpreting it as symptomatic of Britain's north-south divide. Its class war and political stagnation.[5] This was high visibility pop. Jarvis Cocker's stage-protest following Michael Jackson's Christ-like posturing at the Brit awards of 1996 hogged the headlines, spanning tantrums, rock'n'roll weddings and pronouncements on drugs and religion.

Britpop's concept brings to mind the 'I'm Backing Britain' and 'Buy British' consumer confidence campaigns launched by the UK's last elected Labour premier, Harold Wilson. Its pretty tunes bear an uncanny resemblance to those of pop's first much feted 'British invasion' of the 1960. The similarity does not end there. 1960s beat groups blared (Blaired?) out of radios from Land's End to John O'Groats at the same time as Enoch Powell's 'rivers of blood' anti-immigration discourse enjoyed its high water-mark. Likewise Britpop's skewed ethno-historical perspective and union jack imagery makes its ethnicity problematic. Its 'little Englander' introversion and retrogression harks back to an idealised mythical past. This cultural impasse has been parallelled by the Tory 'back to basics' credo and New Labour's flirtation with communitarianism. Fisher (1995) calls it 'at least as disturbing, and nostalgic as John Major's village green whimsy . . . a more-or-less conscious attempt to minimise black influences in music'. In a similar vein Gilbert (1997) writes: 'Blacks, queers and feminists, working class youth . . . the list of enemies-of-Britpop is precisely the same as the list of traditional Labour supporters which New Labour is in the process of alienating'. Britpop has accordingly been unfavourably contrasted with dance music, however, as we have seen internationalism in rave is itself problematic.

By the mid-1990s it seemed that the principle of multiculturalism was becoming increasingly beleaguered with, inter alia, government education advisor Nick Tate's insistence that children should be taught the 'value of Britishness' – taking a very narrow definition of the term. However, the integral element of irony and playfulness in Britpop's theory and practice places it above simply a vehicle for straight white boys with guitars committed to the idea of Englishness. The celebration of Britain in Blur's work is a love/hate relationship with Blighty: a more complex conjecture of textual layers than simply a one way celebration, as can be seen in the album title 'Modern Life is Rubbish'. Kula Shaker, a fashionable whipping-boy of the music press, enjoyed massive sucess with a formula of 1960s Ravi Shankar style sitar-draped psychedelia. This exoticisation of Asian-ness displays some recognition of wider musical traditions, albeit more in tune with the white-ified version of ethnic music that the digeridoos of Goa trance deploy, than the more adventurous 'New Asian Dance Music' documented elsewhere (Hutnyk et al, 1986).

Academic discourse has always valued working-class youth associations of 'the good life' as a powerful subcultural symbol. Music, as boxing, has always been seen as an exit-route from the ghetto. In Britpop 'working-class and hard' is the desired image, to the extent that middle-class bands such as Suede (from Hayward's Heath, Sussex) and Blur have seen it fit to appropriate pseudo-cockney (mockney) accents and intonation in their singing voices. Kula Shaker (of Richmond, Surrey) declined to do so and were much maligned, in large part due their being openly middle class.[6] Blur are graduates of that one-time veritable hothouse of UK pop culture: the art school. Oasis, apart from dabblings in petty crime, have backgrounds in manual labour. However, suburbia can be seen as a common point: Oasis were raised in the post-war council estate garden suburb of Burnage, Manchester. Blur themselves repeatedly celebrated London, and derided suburbia, in their lyrics in a denial of their roots and a glamorisation of the metropolis. If contemporary dance music is rooted in the concrete jungle and Britpop in the village green, or at least suburban angst, urban dynamics are key to both. Rave can be seen to have effected an unconventional sort of urban regeneration. The sites of cultural production are principally located in disused warehouses in the desolate landscapes of industrial estates. A new kind of cultural production in the failed industrial zones that have been deserted by industry.

Britpop's bravado was entirely in keeping with the 'New Lad' climate of the late 1990s. The lineage of its ostentatious masculine tendencies can be directly traced from the phenomenon 'the casual', a refined Thatcherite variation on an age old theme: the lad. Oasis are appearance conscious. Their fondness for Adidas continues the casual tradition of designer labels worn as a symbol of popular consumer capitalism. Simultaneously they project a deliberately raffish image; singing in praise of 'Cigarettes and Alcohol' whilst allegedly harbouring a penchant for yet stronger substances to line their nasal passages. In 1996 Manchester police burglary division were reported as investigating retrospectively some of the Gallagher brothers brags in a recent round of interviews about houses they had 'done' in the past. (*Guardian* 6/4/96) MacRobbie (1996) comments: 'what Oasis does is to explore socially subordinated and disadvantaged masculinities'. Whether the band themselves would put it in quite those terms is doubtful.

Nevertheless, Britpop has seen a number of high profile female performers in groups on a scale perhaps unseen since punk. For 1979's Blondie, the Slits and the Raincoats, 1997 Britpop has strong female role models in Elastica's Justine Frischman, Sleeper's Louise Weiner and Echobelly's Sonia Madan – Madan also being Asian. These performers take actively engaged front-person roles in groups while men play the part of the minstrels. They are also outspoken in interview. This follows on from the early 1990s US riot grrrl movement that was rooted in aggressive femininity as practiced by L7 and Hole. The 1990s feminine model, the 'babe', more gutsy and ballsy than yesterday's fawning violet, can be seen in the advent of the Spice Girls. 'Girl Power' symbolises sexual confidence but it is unlike old style feminism, or at least the negative associations which that particular institution was tainted with in the 1990s, for it substitutes hedonism in the place of austerity. Nevertheless this is a liberated hedonism that would have been impossible without Germaine Greer's 'The Female Eunuch'. These new role models in popular culture mark a reversal of say the 'female dummy' as portrayed in Robert Palmer's 'Addicted to Love' video, where the self-aggrandising male was backed by largely lifeless perfunctory females.

Britpop has provided a badly needed post-grunge impetus to re-establish the British music industry. Pop sales have struck a high note in the UK's balance of payments deficit in recent years. Despite Britpop's independent identifications, many of its most successful exponents are in the bosom of the multinationals – certainly to a greater extent than jungle music. Music's fiscal cake is carved up by the giants who shield the indies. Of the $32 billion global music market, as the situation stood in 1996, 16 per cent of ownership rested with Sony whose umbrella sheltered Oasis (Sony own 49 per cent of Oasis' soi disant 'independent' base Creation Records), a 14 per cent share was held by Polygram whose subsidiary Island is home of Pulp and 13 per cent owned by EMI who include Blur (on subdivision Food records).[7] It seemed somewhat ironic of Oasis' Noel Gallagher to launch a tirade against the 'corporate pigs' of the music industry, given that the band's ascent would have been undeniably steeper without the might of the Sony corporation. In 1996 Gallagher Snr's personal fortune was valued at £7.5 million. (*Weekly Telgraph*, 26/6/96)

Pop's export power, and Albion's raised world profile due to Britpop, serves as a likely explanation for the eager exploitation of it for political point-scoring. John Major did not hesitate to extol the virtues of the 'cool Britania' with the claim 'Our pop culture rules the airwaves. Our fashion has taken over from the catwalks of Paris' (*Independent*, 12/11/96). Tony Blair, always a more convincing child of rock, has chalked up numerous uses of the medium: the inclusion of the

Gallaghers on Number 10's guest list, his appearance with U2 at the Q awards and the adaptation of an Ian Broudie lyric for his 1996 Labour Party Conference speech: 'Labour's coming home'. Failed Tory leadership challenger John Redwood claimed that Britpop was a healthy sign of Conservative Britain, again citing the Lightning Seeds as proof: 'The future's blue, Lucky you'. Nevertheless not even the Spice Girls' endorsement of the Conservatives via the claim that 'Thatcher was the original Spice Girl' could save the party from New Labour's 1997 avalanche.[8] The group's apparent interest in politics seems to however contradict received wisdom of 1990s apolitical youth (Demos, 1995) that launched 'Rock the Vote' (a campaign to mobilise the youth vote).

The politics of pop are more understated than ever before, symptomatic of a decade less direct and more self-referential than ever. The 1990s have seen a shift in emphasis to what has come to be termed 'the new politics' where subversion and opposition are less defined by organised political groupings and more by broad issues that can command support across the traditionally defined 'political spectrum' (Jordan, 1997). Sociological constructs which situate popular music and its actors as locked in a symbolic struggle, miss the point. The defining feature of a different musical type dictates that it must have an accent on separateness, despite music's capacity to transgress difference. The macro Britpop vs dance and even the micro Oasis vs Blur conflicts are healthily in keeping with the tradition of genre skirmishes, bound up with the social construction of personal identity, that have characterised pop history. Social science is the most inexact science of them all. Youth culture itself as a subject is more susceptible to over-scrutiny than most: there is always the danger of well meaning, if patronisingly middle-class, social science researchers being fascinated by the so-called deviant deeds of their subjects. Working-class kids getting dolled up and drugged up to go out on a Saturday night has always been central to post-war British youth culture up to and including both Britpop and 1990s dance music.

Some concluding thoughts

Once upon a time, rave was a verb and not a noun, UK youth culture was in abundant supply and so were its subcultural theorists. Classifying pop's audience exclusively as 'youth', once historically valid, is now admittedly inaccurate; this however is a demographic inevitabilty, not a cause for pop's obituary. Statistics show that music buyers are growing older yet there are multiple, ever-increasing ways of receiving pop's text (PSI 1995). Pop is now only one component of a complex equation of youth culture (di)versions now competing for the leisure time of young people; new technology allows the listener increased participation in their music. Hysterical alarmism about technology, and fears of pop being supplanted by cyberspace, overlook the fact that new technologies are cumulative, not sucessive: they exist alongside, rather than superseding, one another. Music video serves as an example. The industrialisation of music, its movement from a folk to mass medium, has changed its meanings vis-a-vis producers, performers and consumers. Once it was about public performance, now it shifts units, it is background noise even. In all of these contexts pop is an important focus around which cultural identities are formed.

Whether dance or Britpop has 'won' is irrelevant, the two have more in common than might be apparent at first sight; both are among the increasing numbers of categorisations of stock in the average high street record retailer. Britpop for all its problematic ethnicity and musical unoriginality has proved to be an interesting spectator sport. Much dance music is indeed genre-defying if one takes traditional categories as a basis for description, but new musical forms require new categorisations. The wide legion of musical types in circulation today mean that pop is branching out in postmodern directions where people can pick and choose what they want. Both Britpop and dance music illustrate this in their eclectic choices of source material, plundering the past for historical reference points rather than simply looking back in anger. 1990s youth are not an unassuming, unsuspecting public, on the contrary they are a knowing generation. Any new street-originating – for want of a better term – style will be characterised by the extent to which it exists within the shadow of its own past, precisely because it now has a past: four decades worth – from Teddy Boys to ravers. Furthermore to oppose Britpop against dance in a dichotomous 'village green vs urban jungle' battle, as the press have done, fails to realise that there is room for both and indeed for other facets to exist, eg the 'teenybopper' market from which the aforementioned Spice Girls hail. Youth are more than simply a passive consumer group.

Despite attempts to write it off, the level of engagement, attention and meaning invested in music by young people is still unparalleled by any other comparable organised activity in contemporary society. The end of blatant sloganeering in 1990s pop can be seen as a rejection of naiviety for realism: possible with the passage of time. Lamentations of pop's lost ability to rage against the machine overlook the musical resistance to the Criminal Justice Bill – mobilised from the underground by a supposed apolitical generation, arguably with more youthful vigour than the corporate direction of 'Band Aid' in the 1980s.[9] False expectations of pop have the concept of 'youth culture' – bequeathed to us in the 1950s and crystallised in 1970s sociology – to blame for its reliance on the false assumption that youth are an amorphous mass belonging to a generational culture with unitary leisure interests. Britpop vs dance is of little importance because both are on the same side: both are original 1990s pop music by the young for the young, against the voices of critics who are no longer young. Both represent perfect pop in an imperfect world. In many ways in the 1990s pop music is reaching something of an unparalleled visibility in the UK, which can only be welcomed. Pop is still pregnant with value, meaning and power. The relationship of youth and pop in the 1990s can be best summarised, with apologies to Stevie Smith, as 'raving not drowning'.

Notes

1. 'Rock of Ages', interview with Simon Frith by David Walker, *Times Higher Education Supplement*, 1/12/95.
2. 'Bowie starts a craze with a killing on the rock exchange', reported the *Observer*, 9/2/96. David Pullman of Investment Bankers Rascoff Zysblat Organisation who had engineered the deal explained 'I'm not looking for some kid who has just got himself a hot album. We're interested in people who have a cashflow that you can predict.'
3. Personal conversation, 'In the City' music seminar, Manchester, September 1994.
4. 'The food, designers, music, fashion, theatre and journalism make London a great place to live. A hip compromise between the non-stop newness of Los Angeles and the aspic-preserved beauty of Paris – sharpened to New York's edge.' *Newsweek* on London, 'the world's coolest city', 24/11/96.
5. See 'Pop goes the future in a blur of a sound' Pat Kane, *Guardian*, 17/8/96, 'Which Side Are You On?' Robert Sandall, *Sunday Times*, 20/8/95, and 'Pop Goes Britpop' Adam Sweeting, *Guardian*, 8/12/95.
6. 'Why aren't we throwing red paint in their faces, shouting outside gigs shouting "scab", tipping off class war when we see Mills [lead singer

Crispian, son of Haley] down the local Indian?', *Melody Maker*, 16/8/97, on Kula Shaker.

7. Figures from 'Who Calls the Tune?' *Observer*, 25/2/96. Interestingly a survey (reported *Times*, 16/8/97) by the consultancy Media Research Publicity found a decreasing popularity of established acts. Between 1994 and 1996 artists with careers lasting five years or more were responsible for 29 per cent of Britain's best-selling albums compared with 59 per cent in the previous three years.

8. The fact that the revelation came in the *Spectator*, 12/12/96, rightwing current affairs weekly, illustrates pop's placing on a cultural pedstal from quarters one thought to be outside its domain. Also see the *Economist*, 12-18 April 1997, where it was claimed 'The Spice Girls ... have caught the eye of the sort of people whose main contact with pop music is asking for Walkmans to be turned down.'

9. S. Reynolds, 1989 calls Band Aid the culmination of 'everything that was most suffocatingly stable and stabilizing, drearily coherent and anxiously worthy about "rock discourse".' An article of the time concurs: 'Political pop died that day, and the post-mortem revealed a severe case of over-exposure... Bob Geldof was the grave digger', 'Wearing Badges is Not Enough', *New Socialist*, No 63 Oct/Nov 89.

Bibliography

J. Beadle, (1993) *Will Pop Eat Itself?*, Faber and Faber, 1993. T. Bloomfield, WHAT?

M. Fisher, 'Indie Reactionaries' in *New Statesman and Society*, 7/7/95.

S. Frith, *The Sociology of Rock*, Constable, 1978.

S. Frith, *Performing Rites*, OUP, 1996.

J. Gilbert, 'New Labour's Blurred Vision', Signs of the Times Discussion Paper, 1997.

D. Hebdige, *Hiding in the Light*, Comedia, 1986.

John Hutnyk and Sanjay Sharma, 'Dis-Orienting Rhythms: the New Asian dance music', Zed, 1996.

A. McRobbie, 1984, WHAT?

A. McRobbie, 'Lads of Hope and Glory' in *Times Higher Education Supplement*, 8/96.

T. Langlois, 'Can you feel it?' in *Popular Music*, 1992.

G. Melly, *Revolt into Style*, Faber and Faber, 1972.

C. Paglia, 1992, WHAT?

PSI, 'Cultural Trends no 26: Cultural Trends in the 90s', 1995.
J. Redwood, 'There's Always England', *Guardian*, 20/3/96.
S. Reynolds, *Blissed Out*, Serpent's Tail, 1989.
J.Savage and H. Kurieshi, *The Faber Book of Pop*, Faber, 1994.
D. Toop, 'Ocean of Sound', 1995.
A. Ward, 'Dancing in the Dark: Rationalism and the Neglect of Social Dance'
   in H. Thomas, *Dance, Gender and Culture*, Macmillan, 1993.

Discography

Blur, 'Modern Life is Rubbish' Food/EMI, 1993.
Jesus and Mary Chain, 'Reverence', WEA, 1993
The Prodigy, 'Don't Stop the Dance', (1993) and 'The Fat of the Land' (1997)
   both XL.
The Smiths, 'Panic', Rough Trade, 1986.
The Who, 'My Generation', Polydor, 1964.

Ecstasy in the unhappy society

Jonathan Keane

The Unhappy Society: A Peoples History
Chapter 9
The Free Marketeers (or waiting for the feel-good factor).

Throughout 1996, and early 1997, British economic indicators appeared extraordinarily favourable. Inflation was at an all time low. There was an expanding economy and unemployment was falling faster than in any of the countries of the old European Empire. The ruling Tory executive welcomed this new age of prosperity, yet they were uneasy. They could not comprehend why the public were not feeling good.

The Tories viewed British citizens as simple souls. Their actions and pleasures nothing more than a series of rational economic choices. They also believed that their policies had enabled those choices to be made as efficiently, and so pleasurably, as possible. The British people thus had no reason to be unhappy. Yet the Conservatives failed to understand that the British people were not wholly rational.

To achieve their aims the Conservatives had deregulated the labour market. Unfettered by corporate regulation, they believed people would respond to changes in the economy like any good price sensitive product of the period: their wage prices going up and down when necessary; their working hours following suit.

People were straight-jacketed into economically correct personalities and placed under relentless pressure to be productive. Work places thus became surreal environments where employees had to learn to behave and think in a limited way: a repetitive masquerade of treating the customer right, of dressing correctly and of doing increasingly simplistic tasks. Satisfaction for customer and employee alike thus became illusory. Relations between them ordered by a logic beyond their control: the desire to create super profit for its own sake. These circumstances led to an extraordinary increase in psychological disorders across the whole spectrum of working experience.

Not content with reorganising business so that it would run for its own sake, the Conservative party set upon public life. They let the market organise home life, education, service provision and even the social spaces where people conducted relationships. Within this environment people were not free to develop their own sense of identity and they became lost.

The most heinous consequence of this system was the effect it had on the development of the young. Children were placed under relentless pressure to be aware of the importance of schoolwork to their future prospects. They were tested and placed in tabular leagues at every age, forced to encounter the stress of adult reality even before they reached puberty.

Faced with an unstable labour market, the young's fantasies of a better life, so crucial to individual and social development, became stunted by short term anxieties. Discontented and demotivated they began not to look forward at all. Instead they looked to buy their happiness in the immediacy of the consumer present. Leisure became their religion, and for a time, their saviour.

The general public were unhappy despite the apparent good state of the economy, because their well being had been the price for its success.

In the Year of Our Soul 3010

Happiness, the elusive British fantasy

Unhappiness is the cornerstone of British national identity – our emotional unconscious. We pride ourselves on how well we keep it in check. Not 'letting things get you down' is a sign of positive strength and of good moral character. Gloom, an enduring experience of and from the real world, is a solid foundation for worthwhile lives. Happiness, however, is thought of as ephemeral and almost indulgent, a luxury and a fantasy that even money cannot buy. Historically, this pattern of feeling has been celebrated in romantic metaphor, mythologised as a secualrised soul, an intangible ability to withstand adversity, idealised as the 'Great British Spirit'. When transported to such fervoured heights, personal hardship became acceptable and the norm.

We make it a sign of strength, when in truth it is the cultural neurosis that stops us challenging these political objectives which cause discontent. Once the merits of day to day unhappiness were repetitively drilled into British culture by the dictates of the work ethic. Austere Puritan and Calvinistic doctrine coursed through western economic discourse, business and corporate organisational structures. As workers and consumers within those organisations, they shaped our own desires, relationships and knowledge of self.

We remained unconscious of the fact because those same theologies promised future rewards that kept us away from the truth: if we were unlucky in the first life we would be rewarded in the second. And after the rise of industrial capital, if we worked hard we could, eventually, gain Heaven on Earth.

Today, in caring sharing 1990s Britain, the dreams of God and work have lost their seductive allure. The general public no longer believe in Heaven, and employment is no longer a stable enterprise that allows individuals to ignore their present and look forward to a happy retirement. The contract between an unhappy present and a future pay off, has thus revealed itself to be an empty lie leaving a nation suddenly bereft of hope and meaning in their day to day lives and shocked, angry and resentful about the fraud.

The public reponse to the death of Diana, Princess of Wales, was not simply a show of affection from the masses in memory of a much loved figure. Individuals mourned the nation's abandonment of the social good. Tears were shed for unemployment, insecurity, crime, lost dreams. The nation's unhappy unconscious, now unsurpressed, is breaking through in wave after wave of sadness and discontent.

Drugs and me

I first took Ecstasy in March 1994 at Heaven, a gay nightclub in London. At the time, I was working in Waterstone's Booksellers on Kensington High Street. I was new to London, harrassed by unfriendly staff and public alike and only half living on a pitifully low wage.

I went to the club with my flatmate, a close friend. When we arrived she suggested that we drop some 'E'. I was really fed up, feeling isolated and trapped in a boring little world over which I felt I had no control so I thought what the hell and bought, bit and swallowed my way to what I hoped would be oblivion.

Nothing happened for a good half hour. We had taken half each, and cynically I decided it hadn't been enough. I danced somewhat self consciously, eyes towards my feet.

Then a sensation. A warmness in my stomach that spread through my body. After a few minutes I felt a tingling in my neck and then a splurge of gloriously happy energy, steeping my thoughts in an emotional blur of love and excitement. It was as if I were at a concert and music had washed over me with that delicate emotional frisson only some singers can produce, lifting me high. I was ready to slip back down into normality yet each successive surge of warmth up my neck was taking me further into joy.

It was almost too much for me to take. I couldn't remember ever feeling that good. More surprising was that I could think with a freedom that I hadn't known before. I looked at my friend and was able to dismiss much of the normal flatmate angst one picks up when living with someone and see her for the wonderful friend that she was. I could dance in an unrestricted way, feeling that my body would respond to anything I asked of it. I looked around and felt confident to search out the eyes of attractive men. It was like I had been given an intuitive energy that allowed me to look at myself and my environment as it was, without fear, and know what I wanted from it.

The most significant part of the experience came later. A small door had opened in my life and I could see that I was trapping myself in an unhappy job and lifestyle, and that with a bit of work I could be happier. Perhaps not as happy as I felt on the drug, but at least not as miserable as I had felt previously. Three months later I left my job and started on a new career path and the most wonderful relationship I have ever had.

The media's heady quest for youth

The middle classes and the middle-aged feel unsettled about people that have taken Ecstasy. For them, it is a symptom of the unhappy society that they would like to ignore. So they shout angrily, punish as much as they are able, and do little to understand. Their torrent of guilty denial found a suitable totem in the memory of Leah Betts.

Leah was 18, and at the start of her adult life. To celebrate she had a party and an ecstasy tablet. Tragically, she drank too much water, probably thinking it was an antidote to the tablet. Her kidneys in a confused state, could not flush the excess fluid out of her system. Her brain swelled causing cerebral coning, and she fell into a permanent coma. Leah's mother was a nurse and a drugs counsellor, her father used to work for the drugs squad, factors that leant a terrible pathos and symmetry to the context of her death.

Leah became a vehicle for a moral panic. Her face was pasted onto billboards in a nationwide campaign launched by advertising director Paul Delaney. The word 'Sorted' was written large in white on black caps underneath her smiling face. Below ran the warning, 'only one ecstasy tablet killed Leah Betts'.

The press reacted with a quizzical scramble for statistics and surveys so that youth could be understood, contained and told the naughtiness of their ways. The *Independent on Sunday* ran a 'Real Life' supplement, anachronistically entitled 'Sex, Drugs and Rock 'n' Roll'. They announced in a surprised tone that youth are taking drugs in a recreational capacity, 'not junkies on a slow decline into the gutter, not crazed radicals, [as parents would expect] but discerning consumers who decide exactly how much they take and how often'.

Throughout 1996 media youth anxiety bounced off any convenient cultural event; especially the films, *Kids*, *Trainspotting* and *Crash*. By the end of the year their chatter crystallised into a political debate on the containment of young people. Parent-teacher contracts were floated in the public arena and the Liberal and Labour parties succeeded in banning certain knives following the murder of school head teacher Philip Lawrence. By early 1997 the confessions of a drug taking popstar, 22 year old Brian Harvey, were deemed important enough to be addressed by John Major during prime minister's question time.

Youth became victim to sensationalism. They were depicted as monsters, alien to the normal world of the political and intellectual establishment of conservative Britain. It seemed as though the baby boomers who had created this B movie picture feared for their world view. Youth for them existed in a place beyond rational comprehension.

Meanwhile young people laughed in the face of misunderstanding. As Thatcher's and Major's children, their identities were formed in the epistemolgical free for all of the 1980s and 1990s. A time when nothing was true for very long. Their day to day experiences became more important indicators of reality than reactionary and judgemental and moral pronouncements. They are street wise, intelligent realists whom understand the fast pace of our society better than their parents. They knew that Leah's death was not happening to someone every weekend, because the majority had not seen it happen.

Youth culture and the flight of fantasy

In some respects youth baiting is not a new phenomenon. Ever since teenagers appeared on the cultural scene during the 1950s they have been viewed as troublesome. First came the mods and rockers, then 1960s flower children, 1970s punks and 1980s new romantics. Each generation with different clothes, hairstyles, pop idols, politics, and the clubs that gave their pubescent desires a temporary home.

Yet for most young soul rebels, youth culture was a simple fantasy food, with a real world sell-by date. Being young was a series of learning games that led to the prize of emotional maturity and the more complete fantasies of adult life.

1980s and 1990s youth culture is not ruled by the ephemeral logic of fantasy. Nor is it quickly resigned to personal history by fantasy's dogmatic partner, gross reality. The instability and dynamism of the free market has put paid to that. Experiences of job insecurity have threatened the aspirations of young people at the same time as education has raised their expectations. As a result, a fragile, nervous personal sense of optimism has emerged, an 'I'll be OK' response to the future.

Youth live in a hyper-real world where they can buy and sustain the look they want, the music they want, even the type of friends they want, by organising into a visible market segment. Those who cannot afford to do so respond with the same consumerist spirit and create their own complex street cultures and black markets.

In a society judged by market values, youth culture appears more abundant, more efficient, even more grown up than an adulthood that still adheres to a corporatist logic of work and social responsibility. That world, with its increasing economic uncertainties, its incapacity to meet aspirations and its inertia, only partially seduces the young. The hyper-real is larger than life and ultimately more alluring.

To remain seductive this hyper-real culture must relentlessly recreate the illusion of new music, fashion and entertainment. Of course, as victims of the short-term anxieties of the market, producers have no time to create the actual new. Instead they recycle the culture of previous eras, and increasingly the previous day, by simply adding a glossy spin.

Youth are consequently placed in the inert eye of a cultural tornado, and the abundance of goods and empty soundbite information that swirls around them become contradictory, confusing and evacuated of sense. Psychologically, youth are displaced and disorientated, relentlessly thrown up into the air by the promise of consumer fulfilment. A quick fix with an empty culture leaves them dazed and confused and flying back for more. Yet, like the Wizard of Oz, behind its impressive surface this culture has no real stability or power to confer. Not even DKNY ruby slippers can magic the young back to somewhere that feels like home.

With egos built on shifting cultural sands, the unhappy unconscious of young people breaks through. As politics has been seduced by marketing spin it can offer only soundbite alternatives, not enough to keep dissatisfaction at bay. Young individuals turn, in a search for identity, towards the only real thing they know and can control: their own bodies.

I'm ravin, I'm ravin

British rave culture is the quintessential body culture. The music played on the scene is a faceless rhythm and a soaring emotional litany in which the young immerse themselves. Rave was born around 1986 at the beginning of the monetarist boom. A cultural refuge from the chaotic storm of the 'me' decade. Acid House was then in the ascendant, heard at small underground parties. Today it is estimated that 100,000 young people go clubbing every week. Yet the young were never just interested in the music. In this age of extremes, escape strategies need a little help. Ecstasy answered the call.

The drug came to Britain around 1987 via psychotherapeutic and yuppie recreational use in the United States, and the dance culture of the holiday island of Ibiza. British holiday-makers saw its potential for their own dance scene and imported it. They probably never dreamed how popular it would become. Yet they had delivered something magical to our increasingly insecure and depressive country: happiness in tablet form.

Taking 'E' precipitates a surge of love and a feeling of well being by acting on the brain to encourage excess production of the neurotransmitter, serotonin. This canny nerve fluid acts as a sort of chemical e-mail link between the brain cells where memories, feelings and emotions reside. It is also thought to regulate general mood.

Under the influence, takers become ecstatically happy. Contradictory collections of thoughts, fears and neuroses – the mind state of postmodern times – become conscious and connected, yet not in repressive competition with each other. As in Zen Buddhist meditation, a calm order rests on thought, and you see yourself as whole. In the buoyancy of this cerebral positivity you can empathise freely and warmly with others.

The rave scene potentially creates an environment whereby bodies become sources of self knowledge and the ground for identity. A calm counter-activity and a welcome relief from the empty chatter of the market culture.

I'm feeling a little different

> It's like at a rave we create a kind of environment and it isnae just the E that encourages that kind ay feelin. It's the whole vibe. But it doesnae transfer that well tae the ootside world. Oot thair, these cunts have created a different environment and that kind oy environment lends itself mair tae the swedgerush.[1]

The guru of the drug culture, Irvine Welsch wrote this short story, *Fortunes Always Hiding; A Corporate Drug Romance*, about a group of aggressive lads, the football firm looking for a ruck before and after a soccer match. One character Rigsie used to be a core member of the Firm, now he is more interested in love and dealing. He is a figure on the skirts of the macho frame of the story, upsetting the camaraderie of the boys and their little world of adrenalin-fuelled aggro and aggressive commonality with his absent peaceful vibe. In this tale weird love seeps in at the seams.

Times passes strangely in the land of 'E'. Your metabolism is speeded up by the amphetamine in the drug and you feel more alive than usual. Add constant happiness and a background of music with no apparent beginning or end and you have the illusion of an endless present.

Within this timeless environment men and women relate differently to each other. Research has suggested that regular ecstasy use produces lower serotonin levels in the brain. This, it is claimed, can lead to a decrease in indirect hostility and less impulsive and more harm avoidant behaviour. The jury is still out as to whether that indicates neurotoxic damage or glorious evolution – it is probably both. But could it be true that Ecstasy feminises the brain?

Perhaps, but whatever future research concludes, some combination of physiological change and cultural influence is visibly queering men up. On many levels of social interaction drug users exhibit a lack of traditional masculine behaviour: they pause in the policing of male to female difference, show a more empathetic understanding of otherness. Men hug each other when on the drug. They do not feel threatened by gay men, and perhaps most importantly they stop competing. Instead they form their identities in empathy with others. Not from being braver than their peers nor by having a woman on their arm.

This is all good news for our heterosexist, macho culture.

But it is also good for intimate relations. Men find it difficult to get erections under the influence and they feel less active sexually – the nub of phallocentricism happily losing both its cultural and physical grandeur. Both men and women feel inclined to touch each other just for the intimacy of the experience. Sex can become an exploration and a sharing experience rather than simply an identity-defining activity. Women thus feel less threatened by men's sexuality and feel more in control of their own, while men feel less interested in the laddy rush to procure, shag and brag about the trophy. Sex sessions on 'E' have been known to last for hours.

Of course one downside of the drug is that it also impairs judgment. When pissed on alcohol there is nothing worse than waking up next to someone you do not even recognise. After a night in 'E' land you may wake up next to someone you thought was the love of your life only to find yourself with a dirty train spotter from Croydon. Not nice.

'E' has risen up like a bird in flight, a dove perhaps (a symbol frequently imprinted on the tablets themselves) and allowed young relationships to rest on a more humanistic plateau. Out of these utopian celebrations of self comes a feeling of commonality merged with individual pleasure on a scale that Marx believed would come only with the revolution.

Unfortunately the breakdown of competitive masculinity is not something that conservative Britain feels inclined to embrace.

The rule of law

Between 1990 and 1994, the Tory government effectively criminalised young people in Britain. Firstly, the Entertainments (Acid House) Increased Penalty Act of 1990 made a criminal offence of holding unlicensed underground parties. This precipitated a twofold effect on the rave scene. Some groups and organisers linked up with the free festival circuit while other, more money orientated organisers, began to move into city centre clubs.

Outdoor raves such as Castlemorton in May 1992 played host to between 25,000 and 50,000 people. Old style hippy travellers and new age rave kids met here in a strange land of pleasure and self discovery away from the pressure of their normal lives. These free parties were the perfect environments for 'E' and other drug use. Cool, well facilitated, medical care on hand and replete with conversation about philosophy and religion to help direct thoughts and discoveries emerging from the use of the drug.

The government reacted to this new noisy culture with the infamous 1994 Criminal Justice and Public Order Act which made illegal the very idea of rave, describing it in laughable phrases such as 'a gathering...including a place partly in the open air'; it described rave music as a vague group of 'sounds which are wholly or predominantly characterised by a series of repetitive beats'. Unlicensed raves seemed dead on their stomping feet, as, ironically, did outdoor weddings.

Both the 1990 and 1994 Acts politicised many members of the dance culture and they concentrated their energies on creating their own anti capitalist worlds. Drugs were a tool of insight to help form an alternative way of life.

Today, DIY party culture is losing a war of attrition against the police powers granted by the 1994 Act, and their humanism has gone underground. Sometimes the vibe of that scene pops up in the odd warehouse party in London, or the odd out of town quarry. But this type of radical 'E' culture has fled so far from the mainstream you have to have a degree in sociology and an orienteering qualification just to begin looking for it. For the majority this culture is consigned to history.

Legalised drug markets

The type of 'E' culture that is still on the up after eight years is the licensed club scene. The various Conservative criminal justice Acts have unwittingly produced a marketised version of the original underground culture. This is especially true of London, where the number of techno, house, jungle and other music clubs all tailored to a particular youth market segment beggars belief.

Many clubs are highly dangerous; they lack sufficient air conditioning and do not provide access to free drinking water or chill out areas. The majority of the 60 odd deaths from ecstasy since 1990 have been caused by heatstroke brought on by this environment. They are also heavily codified in terms of style – where only the beautiful, affluent and fashionable are made to feel welcome. Poorer youth often sacrifice other parts of their life or turn to a bit of dealing so that they can afford to join in.

The cultural tornado of the consumer world has been let loose in youth's drug intensified realm of experience, along with its addictive empty seduction and fashionable pretension. It dictates that the 'E' user must play out a role just to be a part of the scene. Yet, taking a drug that breaks down psychological barriers in an environment that essentially is trying to build them up, can be extremely dangerous. The combination can amplify anxiety and paranoia in the insecure, and for some troubled individuals, engender a breakdown in relations with reality.

This is especially worrying for gay men who often come to clubland looking for an identity and to fit in to a community. Yet, the majority of the gay clubs demand a simple stern masculinity, body building pumping techno intensifying the atmosphere. Ecstasy use becomes almost de riguer; a requisite accessory to being a proper gay or in a wider sense to being young. In this environment 'E' is often taken by the mouthful just to allow the clubber to feel as if they belong.

A mass anti-depressant is thus commodified and happiness becomes a thing you buy. When this marketised drug world fails to bring contentment the come down can be severe. Work, an already surreal activity, can become a drug weary nightmare. Something to get through before you can once more get your happy, yet paranoid, fix on the weekend.

In these clubs a monopolised black economy thus meets the market economy. It is a world of supply and demand motivated by a repetitive desire to consume and be happy. A perfect combined model of monetarist economics and chemical therapy. Here, Ecstasy use becomes less a tool of insight and more a prop to both relieve and sustain an unhappy identity and an unhappy culture.

Ode to lost joy

There is a poetic injustice in how our society has reacted to the drug culture. Denying any responsibility for creating the need for some mass anti-depressive kick, conservative media and politicians have inadvertently incorporated that need into a weekly market cycle of consumption. 'E' culture is not a passing fad. It is now integral to British culture. The chemical correlative to an unhappy and inhuman way of life.

Our society is reaching crisis point. It seems we can only function with the use of anti-depressants. 'E' is illegal and its long-term psychological and physical effects remain unknown. It has also caused death. Yet similar drugs, such as Prozac, are legal, although equally unquantifiable in terms of long-term effect. They only differ from Ecstasy in that they have been researched and medically sanctioned. Within this contradiction Prozac is ecstasy for the more conventionally minded and GPs are legalised drug dealers.

At some point the fact that the very basis of social organisation in our society produces mental instability will have to be faced. Otherwise we will become a nation of addicts, with all the social problems that embraces. Politicians owe it to us to replace drugs with a talking cure. What do the British want from their lives? How can work and the economy fulfil those wishes without relying on a deep seated acceptance of misery, and increasingly insecurity, for its success? They cannot afford to deny us any longer.

There is a common phrase on the rave scene, that ' "E" isn't as good as it used to be'. Yet many young people are just waiting for the next new drug to come along to see them through their thirties.

The Unhappy Society: A Peoples History.
Chapter 10
What's left for the Left?

Throughout much of the twentieth century, the political left proclaimed its own humanistic fantasy of social relations. Theirs was a communal vision known as socialism and they believed in creating a happier society. At the crux of their ideology lay a critique of the free monetarist market, despised rightly as an alienating structure.

In practice Labour executives failed to tackle the power base of the capitalist deputies and were constantly in thrall to the managers of London City and the rentier classes who ruled that small but important empire. But their vision, their dream, was constant nevertheless.

Their ideals could not have existed without the reality of the market, they were its brave compliment, offering people a way out of the misery it produced. But towards the end of the century the British left, accepted the fantasy of the right and dofed their caps to the spurious realism of business and social relations built upon monetarists economics. Consequently their rhetoric of a new age became trapped in a capitalist narrative. The country would achieve more in the future; but only economically. Accepting the market in its totality meant that Labour could no longer offer the dawn of a new world. All they had left was small talk of softening capitalism's more abrasive edges.

In 1997 Tony Blair, the then primate of 'New Labour', forwarded a rounded concept of the economic actor. Employees and employers in their model did not act rationally towards the market as the monetarists had suggested, but acted emotively. They worked best with people they trusted in an environment that offered long-term stability. He suggested that work should be consequently structured more communally and less antagonistically. This was an important development that offered hope of building a successful economy and which would help people at work achieve contentment by feeling more in power of their own souls. To enshrine this new age of economic relations he developed the policy known as stakeholding.

In one high profile public relations company of the time an administration job provided a salary of £6,000. A graduate entrance job, £12,000. Employees had to work from 9 am to 10 pm regularly, without overtime pay. To keep them happy, the deputies awarded prizes and held parties. A true stakeholding business. Then the next day employees had to work in the same conditions. The pleased smiles on their faces were quickly replaced with stressful grimaces. Not surprisingly, these young professionals were major players in the drug culture of the time.

Stakeholding was a realist dream, a way of making work appear worthwhile. But because it was a dream played out over unchanged working conditions it's duplicity was felt harder than perhaps the failure of former Labour governments to achieve the socialist utopia. It became just one more corporate strategy to increase productivity for productivity's sake.

Because the 'New Labour' government were fearful of challenging the very basis of business and economic organisation they only tinkered at the edges of social breakdown. The mass riots in London, Manchester, Birmingham and Glasgow following the anarchist crack cocaine parties of the year 2010 were a fitting epitaph to this final failure of the left.

In the Year of Our Soul 3010

Notes

1. Irvine Welsh, 'Fortunes Always Hiding: A Corporate Drug Romance', in *Ecstasy*, Jonathan Cape, London 1996, p260.

'That's entertainment. . . ': Generation X in the time of New Labour

Michael Kenny

One of the most salient features of Tony Blair's political style since he assumed the leadership of the Labour party has been his repeated deployment of a distinctively generational symbolism. The imagery of a 'young Britain' about to be born once the yoke of Conservative rule was thrown off recurred throughout Labour's pre-election rhetoric. Indeed Blair's own political image is frequently cast in the mould of the fresh-faced newcomer, not worn down by the cynicism of his elders or grooved in the routines of political life. This stance allows him to present himself as up-to-date in his thinking, and in tune with the political Zeitgeist. It was no accident, then, that he accepted the invitation to appear at the 'Brit' awards in 1995 and has happily revealed his fairly eclectic contemporary musical tastes.

But whilst this may have won him some unlikely supporters (Noel Gallagher was a rather surprising enthusiast) and improved the party's pre-election image, there is little evidence that New Labour has in any real sense 'solved' the problems of youth alienation from the political system. Nor has it addressed the key issue of what 'citizenship' actually means for young people in the 1990s. The apparently unstoppable growth of cynicism towards politics and politicians expressed by younger people has been powerfully coupled with declining participation rates in conventional forms of political activity.

While these trends have been noted and much lamented of late, they have generally been considered in isolation from some connected crises facing modern states. Only an approach which acknowledges and explores these connections can possibly hope to make any headway in this area. And, frankly, there is scant evidence that pr will be easy. Ultimately, the potent blend of youth cynicism, ap, and disaffection with politics signals a deep problem for contemporary liberal democracies; the latter are premised upon cultures and 'values' which are being eroded by the emergence since the 1950s of entirely new kinds of cultures and accompanying identities. The divergence today between 'official' political culture and the cultural forms and enclaves which shape 'civil society' lies at the heart of the problem. The emergence of a massive 'trust gap' between young people and official politics threatens further the declining legitimacy of Britain's political institutions and traditions.

The politics of disaffection

This is not to suggest that the younger generations are simply ignored by mainstream politicians. In fact 'youth' are often granted a deeply symbolic place within the strategic thinking of political parties. Capturing the hearts and minds of young people is a perpetual concern of politicians, and the politics of generational symbolism is integral to Blair's appeal, in particular. In general Blair has played a highly self-conscious game in this respect, seeking to broaden his appeal amongst groups of potential voters – whom the Labour Party might otherwise have failed to capture. The party has gained a raft of new, younger members since his accession to the leadership, a development he has sought to build upon by appointing a Youth spokesperson and creating a new task force. Simultaneously he has proved sensitive to some of the most important underlying social trends of the day. As Geoff Mulgan and Helen Wilkinson have argued, there is an important connection between a fairly pervasive disillusionment with politics and the disenchantment of young people in particular, which most politicians do not recognise.[1] Before the 1997 election, Blair and his advisers showed encouraging signs of trying to bridge this divide, taking his message to milieux and media, where the political parties have generally failed to go. And of course it is unlikely that it escaped the attention of Labour's spin doctors that a fresh and youthful image contrasted rather powerfully with the increasingly jaded and 'dated' look of the Conservative party.

The question of youth alienation from the political process is in fact firmly established on both political and academic agendas. Recent opinion surveys reveal high levels of disenchantment: only 4 per cent of 15-35 year olds, according to a Mori poll, felt that politicians were doing a good job of maintaining moral standards.[2] A social attitude survey devoted to the views of young people found that 59 per cent of those questioned professed little or no interest in politics.[3] Concern about these trends reached a minor peak in the run-up to the 1997 election, spurred by the appearance of 'Rock the Vote' (a non-partisan movement – copied from the United States – which used celebrities to urge younger people to use their vote) as well as a number of opinion surveys which revealed the depth of youth cynicism about politics. To take just one example of the latter, Stuart Weir and Patrick Dunleavy analysed the 'State of the Nation' survey of public attitudes towards the body politic which the ICM conducted for the *Daily Mirror* and Joseph Rowntree Reform Trust in the early months of 1996. Weir and Dunleavy highlighted the decline of trust expressed by young people in political figures as well as cynicism about the motives of politicians:

> In 1973, only two-thirds of people were ready to agree that 'most politicians will promise anything to get votes'; now 81 per cent of people agree. In 1973, just 39 per cent believed that 'politicians are in politics for what they can get out of it'; now a whopping two-thirds of the population hold this view. Belief that politicians care what people think has fallen from 48 to 39 per cent.'[4]

The authors were sceptical about one of the most favoured explantions for this phenomenon – the view that blame can be heaped entirely upon the demoralising effects of the Thatcher administrations. According to Dunleavy and Weir, such an argument might be politically comforting but ultimately ignores a deeply rooted pattern of distrust and disaffection expressed by younger people towards the political 'classes' in general:

> The contempt for politicians is, in our view, bound up in a wider distrust in the political system altogether. . . We asked ICM's pollsters to inquire whether people trusted government ministers and their advisory committees to tell the truth about the safety of food, nuclear installations, 'British beef', medicines and safe sex and Aids. On the first three, there was a resounding 'no' from three-quarters or more of the people

asked. Some 60 per cent replied 'no' on the safety of medicines and even on safe sex and Aids . . . people are still broadly sceptical'.[5]

In the US the idea has long been established that youth alienation is more than a 'blip' on the political horizon, partly because of the much more extensive data available on youth attitudes. Democrats and Republicans are concerned about their inability to attract and hold younger members, whilst some strategists in the Republican party perceive a worrying disjunction between the more 'liberal' attitudes of younger Republican sympathisers (for instance towards homosexuality and abortion) and those of older supporters. The last two Presidential election campaigns have starkly revealed the gap in interest and motivation between 'Generation X' and its elders. Throughout the 1996 campaign, MTV's polling and focus groups (which provide some of the most extensive data available about youth attitudes) consistently found a feeling among young people that 'politics and real life are not in sync'; a recurrent complaint involved the absence of discussion on issues of concern to them.[6] And whilst those young people who did vote, generally did so for Clinton (the Republicans paid a heavy price among younger votes for Bob Dole's 'folksy' campaign style and repeated references to a mythical 'golden age' of the 1950s), this support is clearly 'soft'. Much the same can be said of youth voting patterns in the last British election.

Also in the US, highly developed literatures on voting behaviour and popular attitudes to politics reveal that disaffection and apathy are not new phenomena among the young, though they may have intensified.[7] This is true of Britain too. For example, when Labour lost three elections in a row in the 1950s, a number of 'revisionist' commentators – Tony Crosland most notably – pointed to an alarming gap between the party's rhetoric and the aspirations and needs of younger people. Several critics from the fledgling New Left realised at the same time that younger people had begun to inhabit cultural worlds which were almost immune to the adult discourses of contemporary politics.[8] So it is important to realise that these issues are not entirely particular to the 1990s. Rather, they are rooted in the troubled and dynamic relationships which are continuously being (re)negotiated between modern states and their constituent populations.

The problem with current expressions of concern about youth disaffection is that the interconnections between this and other contemporary concerns has been missed. Efforts to capture more votes from younger people will not therefore 'solve' the profound disaffection which many feel towards the political system. This particular issue is merely the tip of a large iceberg made up of related and longstanding problems. These include the questions of how to integrate younger generations into the political systems of modern states; when adulthood is deemed to begin in social and political terms; how to secure the legitimacy of states in the context of continuous generational change; and, finally, how the political systems of contemporary states should aggregate the different needs and interests of an increasingly fluid and apparently unpredictable population? In particular, we need to consider the problematic nature of the 'adulthood' offered to the young, because men and women have in the last thirty years experienced profound dislocations in terms of the kinds of roles society delineates – as carers, workers and lovers, for example. These 'social' roles were often assumed to underpin the 'political' identities expressed through party allegiance and ideological affiliation, though reality was always different to this. But as a range of changes have eroded and redefined these social roles, they have become the sites of intense argument and social conflict. These developments cannot be separated from the discussion of 'Generation X'.

The crisis of young people's political participation and enthusiasm is not a temporary or easily reversible phenomenon. It needs to be considered as organically connected with a set of other debates and concerns – about moral authority in the home and the classroom, the politics of parenting and the propensity of some young men to anti-social behaviour in public places. Understanding these different questions as related helps us perceive why traditional modes of adulthood appear so fraught and unappealing. On the political left, the question of the 'socialisation' of children into the social world of adults has been addressed by a range of different theorists from varying traditions. But a gulf exists between the emphases of those critics influenced by thinkers ranging from Foucault to Marcuse, who have emphasised the repression and disruption to the individual's personality occasioned by learning the routines of conventional adult life on the one hand, and, on the other, the morally conservative agenda of some in the contemporary Labour party who stigmatise young people as disorderly and threatening – in need of the 'discipline' imparted by paid labour, and a dose of moral correction. A vast space exists between these poles, in which more affirmative and sophisticated ideas about what socialisation could and should mean in the twenty-first century need to be explored.

The passage of young men and women into adulthood, in both social and political senses, has also been problematised by the development of specifically youthful sub-cultural styles. In fact, the density and nature of popular culture may well have critically undermined the foundations on which traditional patterns of citizenship in liberal democracies worked. As Bill Osgerby shows, the emergence of youth-orientated popular culture can be traced back to the pre-war period, but was most marked and controversial during the decade of affluence and supposed 'classlessness' – the 1950s.[9] With the emergence of the 'teenager' and other youth styles, the gap between young people and the established political system was semi-institutionalised. Commentators in the 1950s were as concerned about the apparent proliferation of new 'lifestyles' for the young – vicariously explored in Colin MacInnes' novels of segments of London life – as are many today. What few commentators have observed is that the institutional routes through which the young are socialised into the culture and practices of political citizenship, in ways that complement prevailing notions of adulthood in modern states, may have been fatally damaged by these developments. The 'intermediate' institutions of civil society – schools, community organisations, trade unions, churches and familial structures – have played important roles, channelling social aspirations and shaping identities so that the young learn and reproduce the civic values and shared meanings of the communities in which they live. But it seems that the value systems taught by these institutions no longer enjoy the consensus that they once did, leading cultural conservatives to lament the growth of relativism and pluralism, and 'radicals' to question the wisdom of 'traditional' values in contemporary circumstances. There are different episodes in this complex story of de-legitimation, including the challenges issued by the claims of new social groups and identities from the early 1960s and the effects of the unleashing of market forces in the 1980s. Equally significant are the impact of cultural styles and experiences which make younger people expect very different things of bodies like political parties and make them less amenable to the rhetoric of traditional moral authority.

These issues have crystallised recently in debates about the internet. They underpin arguments about the regulation of access to pornography or extremist political views, as well as the continuing tussle between optimists (can the internet provide a way of renewing democracy and creating new public spaces?) and pessimists (lamenting the individualisation and fragmentation of collective experiences and shared debates). Of particular significance are how these arguments will take shape in the context of younger people. In the US a minor moral panic has grown up around what kinds of information children need to be 'protected from' on the internet – largely an extension of older debates about TV violence. President Clinton has sought to take charge of this mood, arguing for a computerised 'V chip' and encouraging exploration of other methods to empower parents to control their children's access to information on the internet. Some opposition to such measures, and the assumptions that lie behind them, has been expressed, particularly by libertarians. Very few commentators though have seriously considered the possibilities offered by these technologies in terms of the rejuvenation of 'citizenship' and the possibility of new forms of social inclusion for the young. One interesting exception here comes in the form of the 'Cyberkid Bill of Rights' proposed by the magazine *Wired*; as one of its proponents Jon Katz has argued, larger issues are at stake here:

> Children need to be given the chance to develop values and a sense of social responsibility. Learning to make their way on the internet and helping them confront whatever dangers lurk there is no different from countless challenges they will have to face as they grow up.'[10]

The language he uses here is interesting, redolent of much older traditions of civic responsibility and social mutuality (he outlines a contract between children and society, inspired by John Locke's idea of a Social Contract between citizens and state). The question that Katz puts to us is how can these values, which are central to any meaningful invocation of the word 'democracy', be generated amongst generations of young people who are increasingly alienated from the regulatory modern state? Not surprisingly, young people have responded to this situation with the sullen and gradual withdrawal of legitimacy.

The demise of civil society

The decline of the values disseminated by some of Britain's most long-standing institutions has contributed to the erosion of traditional models of masculinity and femininity, propelling a host of new issues on to the political agenda – from the politics of parenting to young male violence. The world of work has long been one of the most important locations where prevailing notions of social and political citizenship were learned. But the institutionalisation of long-term unemployment as well as the deskilling of many young people in the contemporary labour market mean that this arena no longer functions in this way. Those who can find jobs frequently work in low-paid and poorly unionised sectors, where traditional forms of allegiance and solidarity have more or less disappeared. According to Mulgan and Wilkinson, only a third of 16-24 year olds have a union at their workplace, whilst only 42 per cent who have the option have joined one.

The declining legitimacy of institutions like the church, schools and familial structures, and the values associated with them, is undoubtedly connected with young people's disaffection with mainstream politics. This is expressed through low voter turn-out rates and the decline in youth membership of the main parties.

The political parties themselves have tried various ways of orchestrating the allegiances of the younger sections of their populations, and have frequently found it hard to command sustained loyalty over the medium or longer term. In Britain they have relied heavily upon semi-autonomous youth organisations for these purposes. Interestingly, some common features characterise the history of these bodies in the two main parties. At different times they have become too autonomous and rebellious in relation to their parent organisations, most spectacularly in the case of the Federation of Conservative Students and the Young Socialists in the Labour party. The constitutional and political roles allotted to these bodies were the product of an uneasy compromise between the more instrumental concerns of the party hierarchies and wider principles of party organisation which granted relative independence to separate constituencies. Student political organisations too have often become the venues for internecine power struggles rather than creative collective action. Not surprisingly these have provided an ideal training ground for hardened political operators. Frequently beset by the cultures of sectarianism, political manipulation and careerism, these bodies long ago ceased to be meaningful spaces for political debate or sources of initiative and ideas for the parent party. In fact, as was most spectacularly evident in the case of the FCS in the Conservative Party in the 1980s, they at time became self-parodies – the sources of embarrassment rather than strength. Perhaps this was the thinking behind William Hague's recent decision to disband the Young Conservatives.

In terms of young voters, parties have made several attempts to adopt the emblems and styles of popular culture and fashion, and hook up with currents in youth culture (Hague's baseball cap is perhaps the most embarrassing recent instance that comes to mind). This is especially true of pop music. The Red Wedge project of the mid-1980s was one of the more interesting examples of this politics, and 'Rock the Vote' continues in this tradition (though its politics are non-partisan). But such efforts have always proved short-lived and seem to run counter to the tides of contemporary social change. For instance, in a culture that increasingly prizes diversity, the notion of a cultural politics which fixes the loyalty of its devotees to one party seems anachronistic. Equally, the complexity and relative autonomy of sub-cultural styles and practices means that the public sphere is not so much rejected, as bypassed, within the cultural structures of youthful life. Thus there are areas in which young people are relatively culturally empowered, yet the 'capital' they derive from sporting activities, surfing the net or making music means little in the wider social world. And whilst civil society has become more dense and fissiparous, the public domain has in many ways become detached from the institutions and cultures which surround it.

But perhaps the most important dimension of contemporary patterns of youthful alienation which the parties have failed to address is the particularly powerful combination of economic stratification and exclusion with political disenfranchisement. The geographical concentration of areas of affluence and areas of poverty has become even more marked and divisive since 1979. The category of 'youth' tells us little about the even more important differences of experience and life chances which divide young people. Their diverse needs and interests rarely figure in public debate. Where men and women from poorer communities do figure in public discourse, young men are presented as villains, joyriders and dealers – the wreakers of social havoc; whilst young women are allotted, amongst others, the roles of welfare scroungers (single 'parents') and social victims. The realities are, of course, that young people live out a variety of roles and lifestyles in these circumstances, yet find little connection between their daily struggles and the political debates they see and hear in the media. Moreover, the young are figured as objects of a highly moralistic discourse from the political right, which has recently been echoed by some of New Labour's leading politicians.

The increasingly marked gap between young people and official party politics is, however, only one manifestation of a set of fairly complicated changes which have disturbed the relationship between the political parties and civil society. It is not just young people whose loyalties have proved harder to command since the 1950s. The apparent disaffection of younger generations with official politics offers a highly concentrated and more dramatic example of these processes.

'Things can only get better. . . ?'

Some commentators are less pessimistic about these issues. There are more 'optimistic' lines of argument that can be discerned in contemporary debate. First, there is a large social science literature, especially in the US, devoted to the study of the changing attitudes of individuals across different generational phases of their lives. One important strand of interpretation suggests that younger people are always more cynical about politics than their elders, and that this attitude mellows as they age. On this view, 'Generation X' is no different from its predecessors.[11] This argument though has been challenged in several recent studies of youth attitudes which argue that levels of disillusionment and disaffection are intensifying.

Some commentators also assert that new types of politics have absorbed the interests and energies of the younger generation. Theorists like Alberto Melucci, who has conducted studies of the networks pioneered by 'new movements' since the late 1960s, believe that one of the distinguishing features of these forces is their mobilisation of younger age cohorts.[12] This characteristic has been connected with the adoption of less conventional styles of campaigning, a shift away from conventional lobbying tactics and the exploration of new forms of identity – which appear to be central to this new form of politics. And certainly the campaigns and organisations that can be grouped under the heading of 'new social movement' frequently have a particularly youthful complexion. The cluster of interconnected movements which have sprung up in the last few years on green and animal rights issues are, for instance, characterised by their young 'membership'. It may be significant too that surveys of youth opinions frequently find expressions of idealistic concern on a range of social and environmental issues, alongside ingrained cynicism about the possibility of professionals providing solutions in these areas. New social movements tap into these sentiments very powerfully.

While acknowledging that this is so, 'new' politics remains the preserve of only a tiny minority of young people in Britain. Most are unmoved by this kind of political action as they are by party politics. Perhaps most significant of all is that the young have never constituted a coherent collective interest which has been mobilised as a social movement. The varied experiences, social location and values which divide younger generations have rendered this impossible. Moreover, it is simply not empirically true that movements with younger participants are necessarily more averse to conventional political lobbying than other organisations.

A third line of argument which suggests that the picture is less bleak than we might think, stems from the interesting, if still contentious, ideas of post-materialist theorists. This school, most commonly associated with the work of Ronald Ingelhart and his collaborators, argues that generational changes provide the key to some of the most salient cleavages in politics and social attitude which prevail today.[13] Locating a seismic shift in political values amongst the generation which grew up in the conditions of 'affluence' of the 1950s and 1960s, these commentators argue that the emergence of new types of issues on the political agendas of modern states is a direct result of this generation's concern for quality of life issues – now that their basic economic security has been guaranteed – as well as the impact of movements like feminism on young people. Issues connected with personal identity, lifestyle and ethical concerns, or animal welfare, are now supplanting the economic concerns that shaped the politics of earlier generations. Interestingly, Blair has at times presented his own politics in a similar way. Whilst debates continue about the empirical and theoretical viability of post-materialist analysis, it presents an interesting alternative perspective on the question of youth participation within the political system; if Inglehart and his collaborators are right, then the gap between the interests and aspirations of younger people and the agendas of the political parties should close as post-materialist issues penetrate the political system.

This kind of argument finds an echo with the claims of those who see younger people as the 'vanguard' of the information society. Whilst intellectuals still argue about what this term actually means, one common characteristic of their theories is the stress upon the significance of an emerging generation gap between those who orientate more easily to new technologies and older cohorts who have been shaped by the cultures and skills of a now fading 'industrial' society.[14] Much of the more celebratory literature surrounding the Net confidently reproduces the idea of the young as guardians of 'new' knowledge. If correct, then increasingly social institutions and the political culture will have to adapt themselves to the demands of the informational age, and indeed to those schooled in the technologies of the new environment – the young.

So perhaps there are grounds for optimism, particularly in the light of the strategic significance of new technologies in the economy, and the possibility that these may favour the young. Most probably, however, these developments will favour some young people, whilst their counterparts will continue to experience the downside of the post-industrial economy of 1990s Britain – deskilled, casual and less secure forms of employment. Also, the chances of the British polity reinventing itself dramatically in the 'informational age' look poor, given the capacity of our political community to reproduce itself as overwhelmingly male, middle-class and white despite the welter of talent that exists outside its ranks. Certainly an increasing gulf is evident between the atmosphere which suffuses British parliamentary debate and audiences reared on a faster and slicker cultural style.

Social capital and the young

The relationship between the young and the political community cannot be detached from a number of other problems facing contemporary states, particularly concerning their underlying legitimacy and relationship with a more volatile civil society. It is also worth considering how this issue has evolved over time. Indeed a more panoramic historical perspective might be an appropriate background against which to set these issues. In the broadest sense, one might argue that the history of Western Europe is littered with examples of states reinventing their relationship with civil societies, devising new channels of communication, assimilating new social interests and overhauling their political agendas in response to increasingly disaffected outsider groups. Some of the problems outlined here may be unique to the British system, but others are not, suggesting that lessons may be gleaned from other states.

One brief example illustrates this. In the US, one way in which the more corrosive forms of individualisation within young people's lives have been countered is through the ethos and practice of community service. These have gone unremarked in Britain in the debates which have broken out about Etzioni's brand of communitarianism. Many high schools, colleges and universities in the US encourage, and some require, a commitment of service to other social groups. This involves students in a variety of services of benefit to their community. On many campuses these activities are voluntarily undertaken by student organisations and groups to an extent which has no equivalent in Britain. Critics see these activities as a poor antidote to the deeply entrenched economic inequalities which pervade American society. But many young people in the US are at an early stage invited to engage in community activities – working in disadvantaged schools, with disabled groups or the elderly for example – in a way that allows them to imagine a stronger sense of public good, some kind of antidote to the corrosive individualism and privatism of American life. One of the benefits of this kind of experience is that it at least allows a broader debate to begin about what community means, what young people can give to and learn about other social groups, and raises the social value of the participants. This is a far cry from the notion of deference to community values, or the increasingly fashionable moralistic response to social problems which stresses the individual's regulation of her own conduct in line with a fixed value system imposed from above. Thinking about communities as diverse, overlapping and essentially malleable entities should allow for discussion of how young people contribute to the wider public good and the lives of the communities in which they live. This is a very different undertaking to framing youth as a problem of social order which needs firmer policing: better, surely, to shift to a perspective in which young people are regarded as 'agents' engaged in particular kinds of struggle for their own forms of social and political identity, who find the paths to adult citizenship blocked, irrelevant or unappealing.

Re-establishing connections between young people and the political community remains an apparently intractable problem for modern states. Initiatives like 'Rock the Vote' or Blair's appeal to younger people to join the remodelled Labour party are important moves in this context, but unlikely to dismantle the obstacles to a wider pattern of participation within the political system. Debate needs to focus on which forms the political system might devise to secure channels between the state and the wider society, and how political debate can respond to the needs and interests of the different youth communities and interests. If 'New Labour' really means what it says – that it wants to recreate a vibrant civic life – then it must summon the same reforming zeal that it has hitherto focused solely upon the Labour party and open up an agenda here. Young people's assemblies, a youth Bill of Rights, and 'virtual' MPs' surgeries are the kinds of proposals that merit consideration. But more than any specific set of recommendations, the party needs to open a discussion that involves a wide range of public voices and interests, and addresses the connections between this issue and related questions about the apparent crises of adult identity and morality in contemporary Britain. Labour might begin here by abandoning the word 'youth' in its literature and addressing the various communities and interests lurking underneath an increasingly inappropriate label.

Thanks to Jonathan Rutherford for advice on the ideas in this essay.

Notes

1. Geoff Mulgan and Helen Wilkinson, *Freedom's Children*, Demos Publications, London 1995.
2. See *Politics and Voting*, a briefing paper published by the British Youth Council, London 1995.
3. See D.Walker, 'Young people, politics and the media', in *Young People's Social Attitudes*, Barnados Publishing, London p121.
4. Stuart Weir and Patrick Dunleavy, 'The nation in a state', *The Independent*, 23 September 1996.
5. Weir and Dunleavy, 1996.
6. William Booth Younger voters reflect rise in apathy, discontent with politics', *The Washington Post*, 5 November 1996.
7. See for example Jerald G Bachman, Lloyd D.Johnston and Patrick M.O'Malley, *Monitoring the Future: A Continuing Study of the Lifestyles and Values of Youth, 1976-1992*, Survey Research Center, University of Michigan, Ann Arbor and Sharon Warden, 'What's happened to youth attitudes since Woodstock?', *The Public Perspective*, 5,1994, pp19-24.
8. See Michael Kenny, *The First New Left: British Intellectuals after Stalin*, Lawrence & Wishart, London 1995, pp110-113.
9. Bill Osgerby, ' "Well it's Saturday night an I just got paid": youth, consciousness and hegemony in post-war Britain', *Contemporary Record*, 6, 2, 1992, pp287-305.
10. Jon Katz, 'The Trouble with Giving Kids a Safety Net', *The Washington*

Post, 6 July 1997.

11. M.Kent Jennings and Richard Niemi, *Generations and Politics*, Princeton University Press, Princeton 1981.

12. Alberto Melucci, *Nomads of the Present: social movements and individual needs in contemporary society*, Hutchinson Radius, London 1989.

13. Ronald Ingelhart, *The Silent Revolution*, Princeton University Press, Princeton 1977.

14. For an extensive survey of different theories of the information society, see Frank Webster, *Theories of the Information Society*, Routledge, London 1995.

Not such tolerant times

Bilkis Malek

Top of the charts

In January 1996 Babylon Zoo with their single *Spaceman* provided the first South Asian musicians to top the charts. Ten months later Bally Sagoo's single *Dil Cheez* became the first ever song with full Hindi lyrics to enter the top 20. In 1997 Jyoti Mishra, alias White Town, marked the first anniversary of Babylon Zoo's chart topping single with his own no.1 hit *Your Woman*. Success for Britain's South Asians has not been confined to the popular music scene, or so we are informed. Over the last couple of years the British media has painted a (reductive but sustained) picture of a third generation of South Asians enjoying an increasing amount of success in areas where the majority white youth appear (so it is claimed) to be faltering. In education South Asian youth have been reported to be more likely than their white counterparts to stay on in full time education as well as to secure disproportionately more entry places on degree and HND courses.[1] A few rags-to-riches tales such as self-made millionaires Shami Ahmed, owner of Joe Bloggs Clothing, and Reuben Singh, owner of the fashion accessory chain Miss Attitude, have been taken as indications that South Asians continue to capitalise on their entrepreneurial traits and to flourish in the business sector. And, of course, South Asians have always topped the league for strong family values and loyalty to the community which have been singled out as the secret behind their currently revered educational and entrepreneurial status.

This image of an economically successful entrepreneur with virtually impermeable family ties has coexisted alongside another construction, that of a disaffected South Asian youth unable to come to terms with living in the West. This latter configuration, which has manifested itself in a crusade to document and exaggerate a rise in violence and 'fundamentalist' activity amongst South Asian youth, first emerged in the early 1980s following the 'riots' in Southall and Bradford. It has been given a much more forceful prominence following media coverage of the protests against *The Satanic Verses* and the more recent conflict between police and South Asian youth in Bradford during June 1995. Both these almost mythical (and contradictory) constructions have come to dominate debates and commentaries on the experiences of the current generation of young South Asians living in Britain. Whilst neither is able to capture the complexity of what it means to be young, South Asian and living in Britain, politicians and commentators alike continue to manoeuvre between the two. Their simultaneous deployment unveils how Britain has managed to lay claim to a national identity built on 'tolerance' and 'inclusion' without ever shedding its feelings of racial superiority.

John Major's race card with a twist

Politicians on the left began 1997 by renewing their calls for an early general election. Behind the scenes political commentators and critics of the right stepped up their speculation as to when the Tories would play the 'race card'. Meanwhile, John Major was busy packing his suitcase and boarding a plane for a tour of India, Pakistan and Bangladesh. No sooner had he stepped off the plane on his return from the subcontinent than he was on his way to the Commonwealth Institute to mark the 50th anniversary of the independence of India and Pakistan. His keynote address was tailored to flatter and exaggerate similarities between the Conservative party and a section of the voting population highly concentrated in marginal seats. Resounding his favoured public colloquy during the subcontinent tour, the prime minister praised the majority South Asian audience for their contribution to British society, describing their entrepreneurial skills, commitment to self help and strong family values as 'instinctively Conservative'.

A central theme in Major's speech was to depict Britain as a multicultural society characterised by a mood of 'tolerance' for individuals of different races and backgrounds. He painted a picture of race relations in Britain as being free of the racial tension predicted by earlier politicians and commentators who 'feared a trench war between light and dark skinned people' (a reference to Enoch Powell and Margaret

Thatcher). Whilst he made a clear attempt to acknowledge that black people in Britain continue to be disadvantaged over their white counterparts, this was placed within the context of an unfinished job which when complete, would 'make Britain the best place to live'. The hand picked onlookers, predominantly Conservative supporters, responded with a standing ovation, whilst the premiere himself was decorated with a garland. An altogether pristine performance but one which is unlikely to have touched the hearts and everyday experiences of large sections of the South Asian population in Britain.

Major's 'tolerant Britain' is unlikely to have rung true for the young South Asians residing in the Manningham area of Bradford (the focus of media attention following conflict with police in June 1995), Mukhtar Ahmed (permanently disfigured following an attack by a group of white youths in the East End of London), Richard Everitt (murdered near the Kings Cross area of North London by a group of young South Asians in August 1994), and many others who have suffered the worst consequences of racial tension, prejudice and violence. In addition the image of the successful Asian entrepreneur remains far removed from the everyday realities of the vast majority of South Asian youth, in particular those of Pakistani and Bangladeshi background who (along with those of African Caribbean descent) experience higher rates of unemployment than any other ethnic group.[2]

For many young South Asians, perhaps as frustrating as John Major's reductive construction of a British South Asian experience topping the charts in education, employment and family values, was the absence of any effective alternative from the other two leading parties. Unable to offer a constructive challenge to John Major's words, Labour and Liberal Democrat representatives (the most publicised responses coming from Keith Vaz and Paddy Ashdown respectively) resorted to pointing out the hypocrisy of the prime minister whose party has always been harsh on immigration. Indeed those who were eagerly awaiting the conventional Tory 'race card', in order to display their antiracist sensibilities, would have been well advised to take the opportunity to revise their understanding of British racism.[3] For this *was* John Major's race card, only in a language more associated with the left.

Despite popular perceptions of the Conservative party being less concerned for the well being of ethnic minorities, the respective 1997 general election campaigns were indicative of how the current perceptions and attitudes towards the South Asian electorate are virtually identical amongst the leading political contenders. This was made apparent in May 1996 when the leaders of the three main political parties were invited to participate in a programme broadcast as part of the BBC series *East*.[4] The interviewer Martin Bashir asked each politician to outline why members of the Asian population should vote for their respective party at the next general election.

John Major sought to identify similarities between 'Asian traits' and Conservative party policies. In a similar vein, Tony Blair attempted to reveal the appeal of his party to the Asian electorate by claiming a mutual 'ethos and morality'. New Labour's vision of 'a society of ambition and aspiration matched by compassion, decency and support for strong local communities and individuals' was, stated Tony Blair, 'a language very much that Asian people would understand'. Paddy Ashdown began his canvass by stating that the Asian electorate would benefit in three ways from a Liberal Democrat government which would 'provide opportunity', 'a share in power' and 'fight discrimination'. As the interview proceeded it became clear that Ashdown's understanding of the dynamics characterising the everyday lives of the British Asian population was also informed by the same stereotypes embedded in the opening statements of his two contemporaries. When he was asked to explain how his party proposed to reduce the increase in Asian juvenile crime he responded that it would be curbed in the same way as juvenile crime committed by any other group. He added, 'it must be of great worry to the Asian community, a community so far best known in Britain for its stability, its family values and law abiding nature being suddenly infected by the same things others are'.

Implicit in each party leaders response was a pathological view of Asians in general and Asian family life in particular. In this instance, the same stereotypes of a natural flair for business, close-knit family, strong traditions and moral values, successfully used by Thatcher and Enoch Powell to highlight an 'alien' presence in Britain and thereby legitimise stricter immigration controls, were being manoeuvred to win 'Asian votes'. However, it would be wrong to assume that in the 1990s British politics and politicians have moved beyond a concern to control/restrict the presence of black people in this country. The Asylum and Immigration Bill, introduced towards the end of 1995, is but one indication that the 'British' are far from overcoming their 'fear of being swamped by people with a different culture'.[5] In addition a closer examination of the current trend amongst political leaders of promoting 'Asian values and customs' (once seen as incompatible with a British national identity) as desirable national traits, reveals how Britain's politicians have, as Kenan Malik has suggested, appropriated 'antiracist themes for chauvinist ends'.[6]

Behind the lingo of multiculturalism and antiracism

The current generation of South Asian youth have grown up in a period where it is increasingly commonplace to hear of Britain's good record on race relations (better than any other in Europe). Such affirmations largely draw their basis from the fact that multiculturalism and antiracism (and their various initiatives) have become very much a part of the national vocabulary. From the national curriculum to the police force, from equal opportunity policies to ethnic monitoring, never before has Britain as a nation been so keen to project its tolerance of different cultures and races. Yet this national drive to promote a multicultural Britain has not resulted in a reduction in racism. Antiracist and/or multicultural initiatives have certainly provided the opportunity for well meaning people to declare, with much more regularity, zero tolerance for racial harassment and discrimination, and to abhor the activities of extreme right groups such as the BNP and Combat 18. However, they have done little to shed feelings of racial superiority that continue to pervade Britain and the West.

What some have called the 'new racism' has undergone a transition in the Britain of the 1980s and 1990s, taking on an increasingly more insidious character. This transition is captured in the way in which Major and his two leading rivals distanced themselves from Thatcher and Powell in their appropriation of Asian 'traits'. Whilst an essentialist notion of 'Asian' remained very much intact in the run up to the 1997 general election, what has been modified is the way in which 'Asian traits' are currently being appropriated in relation to a British national identity. Once deemed a threat to the 'British way of life', 'Asian traits' have suddenly become the envy of the nation. A key question this raises is, 'Why at this particular political conjuncture has there been such a shift in attitudes towards ' "Asian traits"?' Part of the answer lies in Kenan Malik's recent assertion that 'tolerance', 'anti racism' and 'multiculturalism' have become convenient themes utilised by the state to re-assert a superior (in that it can lay claim to having the best record on race relations), cohesive national identity (in that the nation is united in the fight against racism). Thus, at a time when politicians have become fixed on the 'breakdown of family values' as a major factor in the increase in juvenile crime, drug abuse, and rise in the number of young single mothers, it is not surprising that they have found it beneficial to use the South Asian population, with its 'track record on strong family values', in their respective visions of a future Britain.

By speaking of 'Asian traits' as being in synch with 'a British way of life' politicians may well believe that they can lay claim to promoting a tolerant, inclusive, multicultural society. Two observations suggest that this equation isn't as simple as it is made to appear. Firstly, it is because so called 'Asian traits' happen to 'chime' in with current political priorities and ideas on which to predicate a unified national identity that the notion British is being promoted as being 'inclusive' of 'Asian values and customs'. Britishness has not been revised specifically to include Asians. Rather it is the degree to which Asians are able to display characteristics defined as 'British', that their inclusion within a national identity is endorsed.[7] Secondly, the reductive construction of 'Asian' interwoven into each party leader's attempt to attain the support of the Asian electorate has never captured the complex and diverse experiences of British South Asians. Behaviour amongst people of South Asian descent deemed inconsistent with 'Asian traits', (as in Paddy Ashdown's response to Asian juvenile crime), is explained in terms of a 'clash of cultures', i.e. one culture 'infecting' another. Thus, alongside claims of Britain's tolerant character and good record on race relations are intermittent reminders of the dangers/incompatibility of different cultures living side by side. In other words, if at this moment in British history 'Asian traits' are being mobilised by politicians to convey an inclusive image of Britain, then events such as the Bradford 'riots' have provided the same politicians with an opportunity to re-emphasise and maintain an exclusive national identity.

The persistence in locating and understanding public protests by South Asian youth and their confrontations with state authorities in the context of 'culture clash' disregards the extent to which British racism has been central to the anger currently being expressed. This is not to say that all or even the vast majority of South Asian youth have reacted to British racism in the same way. However, I do believe that the protests which have captured the attention of the British media reveal the intensity of what I can only describe as a 'cumulative' tension and frustration, which has arisen from an insidious form of British racism and not the activities of the BNP or any other far right group. What the state and

Britain as a whole has failed to realise is that incidents such as the 'street violence' in Manningham can no more be interpreted as a clash of cultures or intergenerational conflict as the public burning of *The Satanic Verses* can be attributed to fundamentalist activity.

The source of the deep-seated anger clearly present in the 'Rushdie affair' is to be found in the subtle messages of racial superiority embedded in the everyday language of antiracism and multiculturalism. And it is not specific to Bradford's young Muslims. It is as present in the Kings Cross area of North London where Richard Everitt was murdered, as it perhaps was when four Muslim youths paraded Pakistans national flag from their car on Eid near my parents' home in the North West of England.[8] I have described this anger as 'cumulative' in that it's origins cannot be deduced to one single event or moment, but something which gains gradual intensity from the astute claims to racial superiority that the West continues to assert over the rest of the world. The subtle messages of racial superiority/inferiority occur almost daily but are not so easily exposed and challenged, precisely because they are submerged within an emphasis of equality and tolerance. John Major's speech at the Commonwealth Institute serves as a good example. His repeated emphasis on the 'inclusive' 'tolerant' character of the British was interspersed with comments such as '. . . if you share our love of country. . .'. This token and reductive inclusion of South Asians in a British national identity can also be detected in Dale Winton's comment, 'I bet you've never heard of him', in his introduction to Bally Sagoo on the *National Lottery* programme.[9] Both these instances illustrate the kind of everyday reminders of a marginal and inferior national status granted to British South Asians, and black people in general, by self proclaimed antiracists. In John Major's case, if Britain really was a nation 'inclusive' of its multicultural multiracial population, then would it really be necessary to speak in terms such as 'you' and 'our'? As for the climax of Dale Winton's introduction of Bally Sagoo the fact that most viewers tuning into the *National Lottery* programme may not have heard of this artist is not the issue. The subtext in Dale Winton's introduction is exposed when placed in the context of national identity often being measured with regards to an individuals' ability to recount certain events, symbols, icons, personalities, which have been accorded 'official' national status. Thus, whilst unfamiliarity with Bally Sagoo is unlikely to taint an individuals, claim to being 'British', the opposite is most likely to be the case with regards personalities such as Bobby Moore and William Shakespeare.

Hybridity 'versus' authenticity – not an easy 'contradistinction'

Successive governments of 'multicultural' societies have manipulated the idea of a 'purity of origins' to maintain a national identity which effectively excludes sections of its population. In the aftermath of the 1997 general election it has become clear that within British politics Norman Tebbit remains one of the more explicit supporters of this strategy whilst Tony Blair and William Hague (the new kids on the bloc!) have preferred a more subtle and insidious assertion of the same theme.[10] It has been within such a climate that hybridity theorists have consistently spoken out against all attempts, whether on a national, local or individual level, to lay claim to 'pure' or 'authentic' identities. Such totalising projects, be they the design of dominant or subordinate groups, are seen to endorse rather than relinquish arguments at the core of contemporary cultural racisms.

The argument against the 'purity of origins' fails to appreciate the diverse reasons and outcomes of an individual's or group's desire to ground their identities in practices or beliefs untainted by 'outside' cultural influences. Like mainstream British politics, contemporary hybridity theory has not been responsive to the wide ranging dynamics characterising the cultural politics of South Asian youth. To elaborate and illustrate this point more clearly it is useful to recognise the growing trend amongst young Muslims in Britain to authenticate their Islamic identity.[11] To set the parameters of debate for critiquing the position of hybridity theorists I begin by outlining some of the arguments asserted by Edward Said and Homi Bhabha. I have chosen the work of these two writers for no other reason than that they speak directly about Islam and Muslims.

In his book *Culture and Imperialism*, Said writes:

> Few people during the exhilarating heyday of decolonisation and early third world nationalism were watching or paying close attention to how a carefully nurtured nativism in the anti-colonial ranks grew and grew to inordinately large proportions. All those nationalist appeals to pure or authentic Islam, or to Afrocentrism, negritude, or Arabism had a strong response, without sufficient consciousness that those ethnicities and spiritual essences would come back to exact a very high price from their successful adherents.[12]

Said sees pure religious and ethnic identities as totalising systems which prevent progressive interaction between nation states and different cultures. Thus, any attempts to authenticate one's religious beliefs or ethnic affiliation is a hindrance to the project of building a truly multicultural world. Also, he suggests that in countries previously under imperial or colonial rule the success of nationalist appeals is largely due to the 'untutored' masses at the disposal of the leaders. In other words people who have succumbed to the nationalist appeals of their governments are 'blind' followers. Such an 'uncritical' response is seen as a consequence of an acute desire amongst the 'masses' for a route out of their subordination under imperialist rule. Said deploys a similar framework, a few pages on from the above extract, when he seeks to explain the 'drastic change' in Rushdie's status following the publication of *The Satanic Verses*. He begins:

> Before The Satanic Verses appeared in 1988, Rushdie was already a problematic figure for the English...; to many Indians and Pakistanis in England and the subcontinent, however, he was not only a celebrated author they were proud of, but also a champion of immigrants' rights and a severe critic of nostalgic imperialists. After the *fatwa* ...he became anathema to his former admirers.[13]

Said suggests that this shift in attitude towards Rushdie is not 'intelligible' without reference to a world media system which has, 'through the production of out-of-scale transnational images, very efficiently knitted together the various imagined communities that make up the world'. He is of course referring to the type of sensationalist media coverage which functions to present complex arguments in black and white and more often than not reinforces and invents stereotypes that induce fear and hatred of the 'designated enemy'. In the case of current widespread condemnations and fears of Islam, Said believes that this has been primarily achieved through the overscale media images of 'terrorism' and 'fundamentalism'. Such 'gigantic caricatural essentialisations' are, Said argues, reductive but so powerful in maintaining systems of subordination that the 'enemy' is effectively seduced into a border war which becomes a mere 'expression of essentialisations'.

In Said's analysis of the 'border wars' both sides of the 'them' and 'us' divide are bestowed with a 'blind patriotic' following. The mass support for 'early third world nationalisms' and the stunning aquiescence' of many Muslims against *The Satanic Verses* are just two examples of how the majority of postcolonial subjects are bound together by 'insensate polemic'. Further, because their actions in opposition to or defence of the various idioms lack critical engagement, the resulting border wars become permanently locked in a stalemate. In mapping a more progressive response to what he calls *deformations*, (for example 'the West' and 'Islam'), Said constantly references the work of secular literary and intellectual figures, from the more prominent such as C.L.R. James, Toni Morrison and V.S. Naipaul, to the lesser known like the Arab poet Ali Ahmed Said (alias Adonis).

Like Said, Bhabha describes the dominant reactions to Rushdie's novel as two essentialisms engaged in a battle to claim 'the moral high ground'. For Bhabha an outright rejection of *The Satanic Verses*, authentic religious identities, Islamic fundamentalism, patriarchy and male chauvinism are all intricately linked. This becomes starkly apparent when, having dismissed the fierce anger directed towards the book as the action of religious fundamentalists fuelled by a desire to maintain a 'pure' notion of their faith, Bhabha ventures to activities on the 'margins' to identify the more progressive possibilities of the 'Rushdie episode':

> . . . it's recitation within a feminist, anti-fundamentalist public discourse has received little attention. The most productive debates, and political initiatives, in the post-fatwah period, have come from women's groups like Women Against Fundamentalism and Southall Black Sisters in Britain. . . Feminists have not fetishized the infamous naming of the prostitutes after Mohamed's wives: rather they have drawn attention to the politicized violence in the brothel and the bedroom, raising demands for the establishment of refuges for minority women coerced into marriages.[14]

Bhabha's investment in secular hybrid imaginations as advancing a cultural politics free of racial boundaries is abundantly clear throughout his work. However, whilst he applauds and exposes the initiatives of women's groups as an alternative to the public denunciations against *The Satanic Verses*, it is never clear whether their position towards religion and more specifically Islam is any less totalitarian than those Muslims 'who took to the streets'. Yet, this is something that the reader can only assume from Bhabha's earlier equation of condemnations of The Satanic Verses as irrational, 'fundamentalist' and concerned only with winning a 'binary geopolitical' war. By maintaining a firm distinction between the more publicised reactions of Muslims and those taking place on the 'margins', Bhabha is unable to conceive of women's rights as ever being engaged with by individuals wishing to authenticate their Islamic faith and by implication those who demonstrated against Rushdie and his novel. More generally he is unable to accept any fixed notion of 'Islam' as a liberating entity. Thus, any constructive debates and outcomes become automatically attributed to the position of the secular. This is a tenuous link.

The reduction of Islam and Muslims globally to notions such as 'terrorist' and 'fundamentalist' has been primarily effected through a very narrow media focus linking the dictatorial regimes and armed conflict in some Middle Eastern countries to scenes of public expressions of outrage by Muslims residing in the West. This deficiency and its implications has not been adequately addressed in the work of hybridity theorists such as Said and Bhabha. There is little doubt that the work of these writers has consistently spoken out against the racialising strategies of the West. However, their own suggestion, that political literacy amongst postcolonial subjects is extremely constrained and has been a vital catalyst for the persisting nature of much ethnic conflict, is also guilty of drawing conclusions from isolated actions, events or outcomes. For example, in their respective analyses of the 'Rushdie affair' both Bhabha and Said are right to suggest that the protests against the novel and its author did resonate with the position of certain spiritual and political dictators. And there probably is some truth in the claim that the majority of demonstrators did not read the book. However, it cannot be deduced from this that the leaders from the Islamic world had tapped in to a 'blind patriotic following' to further their own selfish interests. Nor can the anger be taken as confirmation that the mass of ordinary Muslims are submitted to a unitary definition and appropriation of Islam which is inherently patriarchal and intolerant. This can be illustrated more clearly from empirical research.

The primary data around which the rest of this paper is based constitutes a semi-structured discussion with seven young Muslims and a video titled 'Jihads, Hijabs and the West': Young Muslims Speak Out!, in which nine individuals convey their thoughts about issues concerning Muslim youth in Britain. These two pieces of research were conducted in April 1997 and June 1997 respectively. Both were exploratory enquiries and involved respondents from different race and ethnic backgrounds. However, in keeping with the focus of this essay I shall only be drawing on the contributions from South Asian Muslims. At the time of research all respondents were aged between 17 and 25 and were students at various higher and further educational institutions in London.

The accounts afforded by the respondents support the claim that a growing number of Muslims in Britain are defining and asserting an Islamic identity which is free from cultural intermixing. However, this trend is by no means unitary nor has it been in response to the rallying calls of leading political figures in the Islamic world. In fact, contrary to popular perceptions, there were significant differences between the respondents with regards introduction to and everyday engagements with Islam. It is in these everyday negotiations that critical dialogue with systems of subordination, control and intolerance can be found and as such some of the individual narratives warrant emphasis.

One experience that was shared by all those respondents who were born into the Muslim faith was that their early recollections of 'Islam' were largely negative. Shagufta, Ishtiaq and Javed who had spent all or most of their lives in England described why they took issue with the way both their families and molweesaabs had introduced them to Islam.[15] Javed and Ishtiaq were particularly critical of the method of teaching in their respective mosques. For example, Javed recounts:

> . . . when I was younger I suppose I had blind faith. I'd go to mosque and if I didn't get it right, my sabaq like, I'd get battered . . . to be honest I didn't learn because I had so much God fear in me, I was more molweesaab fear.[16] And some of the things he did to me like he'd hit me across the head, he'd make me sit in front of the heater and like bruised my back. At that stage if you wanna learn about something that's not the right way to be taught.[17]

But if the method of teaching left a lot to be desired then this was often equalled by parents' justification of it:

> I said to my mum once like, 'How come you send us there like they smack us and do this and do that to us and even you don't do things like that'. And my mum once said that, 'You get more sawaab and you get more naykee for it'.[18]

It is important to point out that not all molweesaabs subject their pupils to the extreme physical punishment described by Javed, but most second generation Muslims like myself can bear witness to the fact that making mistakes in your sabaq was often punished through caning or a slap across the cheek. Similarly parents also varied in their justifications or protestations of the molweesaabs' actions. It is not possible to comment here to what degree these dynamics have changed or remained true. However, as some of the other respondents were quick to point out they have little to do with Islamic law.

Two main reasons can be identified why those running the affairs of the mosque might assume authority over members of their religious community. First of all the state has not only been happy for migrant populations to organise their own religious and cultural activities but has also been ill-equipped to monitor the conduct of those managing or co-ordinating the respective religious institutions. Secondly, as Tariq Modood points out, religion has been 'central to British Asian ethnicity' although it has by no means eroded or reduced 'the complexity and range of identities'.[19] As such the religious leaders, teachers and spokespeople of some of Britain's immigrant communities have often assumed a superior status over 'ordinary' members of their faith. The latter, whilst not always condoning the (mis)behaviour of individuals in whom they have invested trust to support and guide the religious needs of their families, have not had access to procedures to effect the appropriate disciplinary action. Although, judging by the comments of respondents being discussed here, I suspect that future generations of British Muslims will feel more empowered to hold their religious leaders more accountable for any unacceptable behaviour.

Respondents' recollections of parental indoctrination to Islam revealed that along with the cruel teaching methods of their molweesaabs, restrictive and often patriarchal cultural traditions were also (wrongly) justified through religion. Thus Shagufta contends:

> If I try to tell my parents that Islam actually gives me the right to marry another Muslim whether he's black or white or whatever they won't like it. It's like if I say 'No mum I don't have to wear red on my wedding day it's not Islamic', and she just can't understand it.'

For Shagufta, distinguishing cultural traditions from religious requirements has become necessary in order to challenge some of her parents' expectations with regards her selection of marriage partners, dress and so on. Confronting patriarchal and sexist practices was also central to Ayesha and Noshin's childhood experiences and their own dialogues with Islam. Though born in England both Noshin and Ayesha, who are sisters, had spent most of their childhood and teenage years in the Middle East. They had lived eight and a half years in Bahrain, and a total of five years in Saudi Arabia of which two were in Arbir and three in Jeddah. Both sisters had expected more stricter regulations of public behaviour in Saudi Arabia compared to what they had been used to in Bahrain which resulted in protestations to their parents:

> N: . . . when we actually went to Jeddah we were so adamant. We were just like, 'We hate it here, we're not going to like it, we can't like it'.
> A: Yeah like, 'There's no way that you're going to make us wear hijab!'

The determination of the sisters to resist any significant changes to their own lifestyles proved difficult, as Noshin discovered on her first day at school.

> What happened was the first day I actually went there I was in my tight jeans and hairspray in my hair and everything (group laugh) . . . and as I'm leaving I get this whack (describes with hand) on the back. And I turned round and this woman goes, 'Are you Muslim?' And I go, 'Yes I am'. She goes, 'Why isn't your hair covered? Where's your rabbiah?', you know the black thing you wear. And I'm just like, 'My God', I go, 'Look I'm really sorry I didn't know it was part of the school regulations. There's no need for you to hit me'. You know and I was like, 'From tomorrow I'll wear one'.

In spite of their respective disquieting introductions to Islam many respondents have in recent years become committed to authenticating and defending their faith. Leila Ahmed, in her book *Women and Gender* in Islam, distinguishes between the different forms this attachment to Islam may take.

Ahmed differentiates between 'establishment' or 'pragmatic' Islam and 'ethical' Islam. She highlights how these are 'two distinct voices' and 'two competing understandings of gender'. The establishment version is the Islam of the politically powerful which promotes an androcentric vision and 'has been extensively elaborated into a body of political and legal thought, which constitutes a technical understanding of Islam'.[20] By contrast, ethical Islam 'has left little trace on the political and legal heritage of Islam'.[21] However, it is this second voice of Islam that carries an 'egalitarian conception of gender' and is a consistent feature in many of the passages of the Quran. This is in fact a marked distinction 'from the scriptures of other monotheistic traditions, in that the Quran not only explicitly addresses women but also accords them absolute moral, spiritual and biological equality'.[22]

That both versions have coexisted alongside each other, even in Mohammed's own practices, is indicative of 'how Islamic and Arabic cultures, no less than the religions and cultures of the West, are open to reinterpretation and change'.[23] It is not possible to detail here how the balance of emphasis and tensions between the two readings of Islam has changed throughout history, for different societies and between individuals. However, a small example provided by Ahmed, illustrates the extremity of the positions that might result from the two interpretations.

> . . . verses such as those that admonish men, if polygamous, to treat their wives equally and that go on to declare that husbands would not be able to do so – using a form of the Arabic negative connoting permanent impossibility – are open to being read to mean that men should not be polygamous.[24]

Applying a more ethical interpretation of Islam, particularly in relation to challenging patriarchal and nationalist attitudes, was central to the religious identities being negotiated by many of the respondents in my own empirical research. This became apparent from the reasons they offered in explanation for the reversal in the trend from disregard or marginalisation to a desire to authenticate their religion. These can be summarised under three broad areas. Firstly, as was hinted at in the earlier quote from Shagufta, parents often tried to impose or pass cultural traditions as religious requirements. In Imran's words:

> The fusion of Islamic culture with Asian culture or Pakistani culture has led to the blackening of the name of Islam.

Shagufta repeatedly found that, by separating out the multiple cultural influences embedded in her parents' religious position she was much more able to challenge their justifications:

> When I was younger when people used to come round my mum used to give me like a dupatta just a thin piece of cloth and which you could see through. And she'd be like 'Wear this when people come round'. But if

I was to actually put on a proper thing she would have freaked out, she'd
be like 'What you doing?!'

Another factor why young Muslims have wanted to ground their faith
is related to the ways in which Islam in Britain has been manipulated
to re-establish national and cultural boundaries that have been
disrupted by migration. A prime target for this, as some individuals
recounted, was the method of calculating the day on which Eid is celebrated.[25] For example, if they are aware that Indian Muslims will be
observing Eid on the 30th day, some Pakistani Muslims will fast an
extra day (regardless of whether the moon has been cited) as a way of
maintaining distinctions in their national origins (and vice versa). Such
nationalist divisions are also confirmed and compounded by the fact
that membership of local mosques is often heavily influenced by country of origin. By adhering to the directions of the Quran and hadith
that are not open to interpretation, it has been possible for many young
Muslims to dissociate themselves from the nationalist rhetoric and
tensions that are played out between the different Muslim communities, and which members of their own families might be engaged in.

The third dynamic contributing to what some have termed, 'the
Islamic revival', is that many individuals have not felt adequately
equipped to successfully negotiate their way through the demands of
living in a postmodern society. Respondents felt a distinct uneasiness
with experiences of fragmentation and chaos. As Noshin succinctly
puts it:

> In this increase in secularisation we don't have the perceptual tools to
> gauge with, there not being one unified truth or what have you. So
> perhaps like young Muslims turn to Islam as a sort of thing to hold on
> to, a sort of anchorage or certainty.

At this stage it is appropriate to point out that the significance and
combination of the reasons cited above varied for each individual.
Accordingly there was no unitary position or observance of Islam
amongst the respondents. However, by returning to the passages of the
Quran and hadith many young Muslims in Britain have been able to
foreground and practise an ethical interpretation of Islam, one far
removed from many of the systems endorsed by establishment Islam
and which continue to inform the policies of many governing elites in
the Islamic world. The framework within which dominant discourses

in the West have tended to make sense of the lives of Muslims remains firmly rooted in establishment Islam. The growing antagonism currently being expressed against the hijab is indicative of this situation.

In Britain, as in some other European countries, the veil, in its various forms, has become much more visible in recent years. Its growing prominence has once again brought to the fore phobic reactions against Muslim identities. These have ranged from the ban on veiling enforced by French schools, to the more mundane public reactions which, as Ayesha's mimicking summary suggests, cannot accept an articulate, assertive, intelligent woman wearing a hijab as anything other than a contradiction:

> A major problem in British society is that there's a huge huge demonisation of Muslims and there's a tendency to put us in uniformed categories. Like, Muslim woman, dressed in black. Covers her face, covers her hair. No identity, isn't allowed to speak. So, when your sitting on the train and your reading a newspaper or a good book or even if your writing, people sort of look and they're just like, 'Ugh she can write and she can read. And she reads intelligent stuff! And oh my God!'

Veiling in Muslim societies and by Muslim women is very complex and I do not have the time to go into any detail here. However, I have failed to understand why in the West there is a blind spot when it comes to accepting that people may find as much freedom in covering their bodies as others do in revealing, tattooing or piercing their bodies. Much depends on how the individual perceives and negotiates their surrounding environment and what makes them feel the most liberated and at ease in relation to notions of sexuality or gender relations. For some Muslim women veiling has become an important part of that negotiated position. Neither populist nor radical Western thinking has been able to accept this basic fact. More importantly the unlocking of the current 'border wars' between 'Islam' and the 'West' is to some degree dependant on a global recognition that Muslim lifestyles can be as capable and committed, as the aspirations of secular liberals, in embracing the ideals of human freedom, equality and justice.

The empirical data presented here is by no means representative of all South Asian Muslims in Britain. Indeed the research has barely touched on the spiritual dialogues taking place amongst the respondents themselves. As such it would be wrong to conclude that their respective negotiations and appropriations of Islam are unproblematic on all accounts. My aim here has been to draw attention to the fact that within their everyday negotiations there exists an undeniable commitment to distance themselves from the more pragmatic appropriations of Islam. It is these everyday negotiations that need to be tapped into and given space for public expression if the more prominent voice and images of establishment Islam are to be effectively challenged.

The framework within which writers such as Said and Bhabha have sought to analyse the 'polemical' reactions of Muslims to *The Satanic Verses*, is perhaps closer than they would like to concede to the way British politicians have made sense of the identities being forged by South Asian youth. In drawing their conclusions about a 'purity of origins' from isolated events such as the 'Rushdie affair' hybridity theorists may have forfeited important ground in challenging the 'rise of Islamophobia in the West'.[26] On this issue New Labour recently confirmed its reluctance to exercise its powers to help protect the rights of Britain's Muslim citizens when the Home Secretary, Jack Straw, announced that a new law banning religious discrimination was highly unlikely in the lifetime of this parliament. Perhaps then they'll also put multiculturalism on hold until after the next general election!

Moreover, as the preceding discussion suggests, the commitment to negotiating a more humane, anti-nationalist, anti-racist way of life is not the exclusive propriety of only the secular imagination. With that in mind and in order that South Asian youth may be truly incorporated into their respective visions of multicultural Britain, both hybridity theorists and New Labour will need to radically revise their current approaches to racial and cultural identities.

Notes

1. A survey quoted in the programme titled 'Relative Values' (broadcast on 24th April 1996 on BBC 2) indicated that 79 per cent of all South Asians aged 16-19 yrs remained in full time education compared to 57 per cent of Whites. In addition although South Asians only constitute 2.7 per cent of the population, they occupy 6 per cent of all degree and HND places.
2. Figures for spring 1995, collated by the Labour Force Survey, indicate that the unemployment rates across Great Britain for the 16-24 age group were 39 per cent for the two categories 'Pakistani/Bangladeshi' and 'Black'; 23 per cent for 'Indian' and 14 per cent for 'White'.

3. See for example John Sweeney's article 'Major Rises Above Mockery In Bid To Become Man of All Races' published in *The Observer* on 19th January 1997. Also see leader comment on p23 in the same issue.

4. The programme titled 'A Power in the Land' was broadcast on 29 May 1996 on BBC 2.

5. The Asylum and Immigration Bill introduced a 'white list' to indicate countries (including Pakistan, India, Sri Lanka and Nigeria) from where applications for asylum may still be assessed, but would in the first instance be accepted as being from 'safe' countries and therefore likely to be bogus.

6. See chapter 5 'Cultural Wars' in K. Malik, *The Meaning of Race*, MacMillan Press Ltd, London 1996.

7. This is further supported by the fact that despite invitations by the organisation Operation Black Vote the leading politicians did not make themselves so visible amongst the African Caribbean population. Perhaps given their current priorities of strong family ties and economic growth it has not been so easy to accommodate their understanding of 'African Caribbean traits' within their vision of Britain.

8. The body language of many onlookers suggested that they were infuriated by this act. Clearly a very different response from the one drawn by the parading of the Union Jack during events such as VE day and England's World Cup victory against Holland during Euro '96.

9. Broadcast on 11 January 1997 on BBC1.

10. At a fringe meeting at the 1997 Tory party conference Norman Tebbit reaffirmed his doubts about multiculturalism suggesting that it was another 'Bosnia' waiting to happen! Meanwhile on centre stage William Hague opted for his predecessor, John Major's approach, expressing a concern for the lack of black and Asian members.

11. In the context of this essay, it is important to note that although Islam is not the religion of all British South Asians, as Avtar Brah points out: 'Racism against South Asians in ... the late twentieth century ... represents a reconstitution of 'the Asian' ... through the foregrounding of 'the Muslim', in A. Brah, *Cartographies of Diaspora*, Routledge, London 1996, p169.

12. E. Said, *Culture and Imperialism*, Virago, London 1993, p371.

13. *Ibid.*, p373.

14. H. Bhabha, *The Location of Culture*, Routledge, London 1994, p229.

15. Teachers at the mosque are referred to as molwees or mloweesaabs.

16. 'Sabaq' means the homework given by the molwee. This usually constitues learning to read a passage from the Quran in Arabic which is then read out to the molweesaab. Emphasis is on pronunciation of Arabic.

17. It should be highlighted that the kind of mosque and classroom teaching being described by Javed is specific to Muslim organisations that provide evening classes for children primarily for learning to read the Quran in Arabic. They have a different set up and purpose than the Muslim schools in Britain. The latter tend to be much more professionally organised, have a certified curriculum and do not resort to the teaching methods of the former.

18. 'Sawaab' and 'naykee' are both terms used to suggest that in return for certain deeds or actions you will be rewarded positevely in 'janat' (i.e. Allah's house) or that your passage to 'janat' will be easier.

19. T. Modood, 'Difference, Cultural Racism and Anti-Racism' in P. Werbner, and T. Modood (eds), *Debating Cultural Hybridity*, Zed Books, London 1997, p158.

20. L. Ahmed, *Women and Gender in Islam*, Yale University Press, New Haven 1992, p66.

21. *Ibid.*

22. *Ibid.*, p64

23. *Ibid.*, p245.

24. *Ibid.*, p63.

25. If the moon is cited on the 29th day of Ramadan then Eid is celebrated on what would have been the 30th fast. If the moon is not cited on the 29th then an extra day of fasting is required and Eid is celebrated the day after.

26. Runnymede Trust, *Islamophobia: A Challenge for Us All*, 1997.

Reading identity: young Black British men

Elaine Pennicott

> We are shut out of so many areas like TV which is such a powerful medium, so that our stories are told for us. . . . With books it's a lot easier especially if you have got companies like X Press. We have got so many stories that haven't been told that it's (writing) also a way of communicating . . . even if I can't be there to take part in the conversations, I feel I am able to communicate.
>
> Yana Richardson, interview 16/08/96

The idea that there exists a knowable 'Black youth' seems obvious. Leading figures across the political spectrum such as Police Commissioner Sir Paul Condon, Labour MP Kate Hoey, radical black organisations such as Panther, all claim an intimate knowledge of the truth about 'Black youth' – mugger of old ladies, rioter, illegal immigrant, drug dealer, athlete, problem of the inner cities, rebel, soul brother, funkateer. The otherness of black masculinity has been narrated through these apocryphal myths. It has been perceived as a problem, something which is at odds with, and on the margins of, British society, and which cannot be incorporated into definitions of Britishness. Black men have been labelled, discussed and viewed as a problem that needs sorting out.

Writing about colonised subjects in France in the 1950s and 1960s, Frantz Fanon, in *Black Skin White Masks*, noted that in the colonial imagination, the Negro was less a person and more a public site on which different fantasies and fears were played out. The Negro he argued, didn't really exist outside of the stereotypes that circulated knowledge about him to the general French population. The myth of 'Black youth' today functions in a similar way. It tells more truths about the fears and fascinations of our society than it does of young people of colour living in Britain. Myth operates as a sort of public space – a territory of representation that is at times remarkably familiar but at others quite alien, yet distinctly and uniquely British. The myth of 'Black youth' has very little to do with individual young black men. It is a place they visit along with the rest of the British population, but one they are forced to occupy when the dominant white gaze is upon them.

Party politics at the end of the 1990s continues to indulge these myths. New Labour's successful attempt to occupy the middle ground of British politics has reinforced the marginalisation of groups which do not occupy 'Middle England'. The 'conservative modernity' proposed by Blair with its reassertion of the family and social values relies upon an image – as did Enoch Powell's and Margaret Thatcher's – of the violent inner city inhabited by hostile outsiders, in particular unemployable black youth: sexually irresponsible, potentially violent, and demanding valuable resources from an embattled state sector.

I am particularly interested in how young people of colour respond to these myths, which have dominated public spaces of representation for so long and which constantly demonise and marginalise them. For the stories they tell about themselves are more interesting and revealing than the stories that are told about them. The mainstream and the political parties, with their narrow understanding of what it is to be British, do not see the many ways in which young black men engage in everyday, ordinary British life. Their lives have been ignored except when they coincide with dominant myths of 'Black Youth'. Then they become examples of 'we told you so', for that is 'obviously' and 'naturally' what they are like.

The emergence of a Black British popular literature demonstrates the extent to which young black people take part actively, albeit less formally and less visibly, in British cultural and political life.

The fiction of young black people represents a fertile and popular place of aesthetic and political expression. The literature documents the desires, pleasures and pain of living in modern British society, and how young Britons of colour refuse to engage in any simplistic way with the dominant images and myths about themselves. The persistent narratives of 'Black youth' are considered, tried on for size, and played with, rather than simply being adopted or rejected. Popular fiction, like music, photography and film, is a symbolic place where myths of and about black youth can be reenacted, challenged and reconstituted. In the 1990s it is an important element in this performance. It provides a site which is more or less outside of the control the dominant forms of fiction and publishing, and where young Black Britons can more freely tell their stories, express their creativity and set up conversations with others. This article is based on interviews with two influential figures in black writing and publishing – Diran Adebayo winner of the 1996 Saga prize for literature with his novel *Some Kind of Black* (Virago 1996), and Doton Adebayo, who with Steve Pope set up the publishers X Press.

The Yardie myth

X Press began producing popular literature written by black authors for black audiences in the late 1980s. Their books were an immediate success, particularly *Yardie* by Victor Headley, which has since become a trilogy. *Yardie* is an old fashioned and rather moralistic gangsta tale set around Brixton, Hackney and Finsbury Park. It tells of illegal immigrants, drug dealing and gang warfare. Targeted specifically at young, metropolitan black people, it was initially sold outside clubs and dance halls and in local newsagents. The success of *Yardie* (1992) and Augustus Patrick's *Baby Father* (1992), resulted in the sale of film rights to the BBC, the sale of publishing rights to Pan Books, and the expansion of X Press's catalogue to include young unknown black British authors. Subsequently large book shops, such as W.H. Smith, created specific sections for Black literature. Dotun Adebayo says of this time:

> Within something like 9 months we sold 12,000 copies, of which maybe half of that was through bookstalls and the other half was through non-book outlets, whether it was us directly selling them or via a pattie shop, or a hairdressers or a record store or whatever.... now we take for granted that when we go to WH Smiths, or at least to a WH Smiths in a black area, we are going to see a stand for black interest books. (interview 16.8.96)

Yardie quickly entered into the wider popular imagination. *The Independent, Daily Mail* and the *Observer* all carried features on Headley and the 'Yardie drug culture', with headlines such as 'Yardie's Evil' and 'New racism finds a Yardie stick'. The novel was seen as an index of the black population in general, and black men in particular. Headley was reviewed as simply telling the truth about black life in London. The *Hackney Gazette* wrote: 'he admits the authentic detail of the novel comes from an intimate knowledge of the secret wheeling and dealing of the gangsters... totally accurate representation of the Yardie drugs scene in Hackney'.(29.6.92) The novel was supposedly so 'real' that Headley had to leave the country after it was published, in fear of retribution from those in London who thought he 'knew too much'. It is also reputedly recommended reading at the police training school in Hendon. Whether this is fact or myth, it indicates the extent to which *Yardie* entered the public realm of fantasy and myth about black men and inner city life.

Yardie came to exemplify 'Black youth' as a vilified version of young masculinity. The right-wing media condemned Headley and X Press for advocating violence and drug dealing. But black organisations also condemned the reproduction of negative, racist images of the black community. Publisher Doton Adebayo comments on this tension:

> There are stereotypes within our community, but I don't know anybody who is in the business to produce them, that would be suicidal, unless you are saying that our readership is so stupid that they can't see through stereotypes. They see them every day. The same people that write the books are reading the books. They are ordinary people, they choose the topics to write about, they write about them from black perspectives.

The myths that circulated about *Yardie* delimited the space of cultural imagination which framed the knowledge of young black men. For Doton, stories are a crucial way in which Black Britons can give form to the contradictory and often painful experience of living in modern Britain and he dismisses the attempts to reduce the different concerns and expressions of identity to a one dimensional image. Literature is an essentially political practice. Young black men, he asserts, are engaged in complex negotiations with other black men, with women, with white people, as well as with the myth of Black youth – negotiations that are taking place on many different sites. The response to the book revealed more about popular perceptions of black masculinity than it did about the lives of young black men.

Black flaneurs

'Black youth' is articulated within a rhetoric and fear of Americanisation: images of hoods, crack dealers and street killings.

British Black youth is defined in relationship to this dystopia of the American inner city. The work of French poet Charles Pierre Baudelaire (1821-1867) proves useful for prizing free young black British men from this stereotypical habitat. Baudelaire evoked a mythical Paris, one which celebrated the dislocation and the unsettling experiences of modernity. The natural inhabitant of this modern city was the *flaneur* who, picking his way through the streets and spaces of the city, learnt to master it. 'Black youth' can be reinterpreted as modern day flaneurs or dandies, who live outside the anachronistic fantasy called middle England – in a place that is always constructed as other to the respectable. Baudelaire's vision of the city, with its sense of decay, from which lives and loves can grow, constructs subjects who do not fit easily into the stereotypes of good and bad. Rather they become implicated in the fears and fantasies that attempt to define them.

Victor Headley writes about this modern day flaneur and maps out his city. His characters D, Piper, and Charlie parade the streets of Hackney and Brixton in their meticulously chosen clothes. They know London, its hidden dance halls and drinking places. The London they inhabit comes to life at night when ordinary citizens are in bed, and the London bobby is replaced by the vice and serious crime squads. D is an outsider, the antithesis of 'middle England'. His codes of behaviour and language can only be understood by those who share his metropolis. D lives on the margins, running gangs and dealing drugs. In a strange way D represents the working-class hero who, struggling against the violence and prejudice of his society, comes to master it.

Diran Adebayo writes about a different city, but it is still one in which modern flaneurs inhabit the street – that mythical place. *Some Kind of Black* tells the story of Dele, an Oxbridge student who inhabits a paradoxical world, part of the elite of British society, and part of the Brixton street. Unlike D in *Yardie*, Adebayo's main characters come from Nigeria. Adebayo's writing demonstrated a keen awareness of the myth of 'Black youth', yet he refuses to be defined by it. His is a London inhabited not by gangstas but by different 'selves' in negotiation and conversation with each other: 'you get a very sharp sense of how identity isn't static at all but is made up of your reactions to the kinds of selves you have to be'.

He writes of a city that is not simply where those outside respectable British society live but a London where young men play with different identities and perform their masculinity depending on the social and cultural context; be it a 'little ghetto jive' to attract a pretty, middle-class Oxford student, or acting the 'original gentleman' to a pretty 'home maker rather than butt-shaker'. Adebayo shows how in the city, young men engage with the dominant myths of black people, which places them in centres such as Brixton, that insist they are Jamaican, that they all came over here in the 1950s, that they are not academic and so on – what he calls the orthodoxy of black life. His writing engages with the complex and ambivalent ways in which young black men negotiate the experience of modern life, of police violence, of the demands of parents who emigrated to England with dreams and hopes but watched as they withered, of childhood friends who chose to conform to the low expectations of them held by British society.

Unlike Headley who is sited in the marginal, mythic black areas of London, Adebayo is much more unsure of his place in London:

> I find it difficult in terms of where to live in London because I am a member of a lot of different homes. Maybe more homes than most people have in a sense – I'm kind of from Nigeria but I haven't actually been to Nigeria, so I can't have an automatic claim to various Nigerian heartlands like north west London as other people do . . . [also] private school . . . obviously black. I feel a bit off centre, its just kind of difficult to find a place where I can feel that yes, this is my area.

Adebayo cannot write with certainty about his place in London because like other young black men he cannot easily fit himself into the stereotypical images or areas of black masculinity. He is uncomfortable with the orthodoxy of black life, because it forces him to enact a role which is partly alien to him. Whilst he is black, he is not Jamaican; he walks the streets late at night, but he does not sell drugs. The approval of his father is deeply important to him (and to Dele in the novel), yet his values are different. But the orthodoxy is still deeply attractive. It provides a way in which black men can communicate through a short hand of shared experience – on the one hand of excessive social attention, for example from the police, yet on the other the invisibility of everyday, institutional and local racism.

What is clear from the examples of Headley and Adebayo is that young Black British men refuse to engage in any simplistic way with the dominant images and myths about them. Their identities are not fixed by history or biology, but like all identities, are performed and acted out in relations to the many different cultural and political contexts they find themselves in. The idea that there is a knowable

'Black youth' is constantly challenged and refuted by a performativity which questions its mythology. Black men going to Oxford University, black men staying at home to look after their children, Black men who know and respect their fathers. The urban spaces that these men inhabit may not be recognisable to the dominant white British society, but it is a mistake to assume that they, therefore, do not exist.

The benefits of work?: lone motherhood under New Labour

Karen Triggs

Lone parents are getting younger. In recent years there has been a rise in the proportion of lone parents under 25, who now form a fifth of all lone parents. Many of these young lone parents are the unemployed single mothers of popular myth, in receipt of income support and other state benefits as they care for their children. The Government's New Deal for lone parents, a scheme designed to assist lone parents with a search for work, hopes to cut the number of lone mothers on the dole. But can it really help the increasing numbers of younger unemployed lone mothers get back to work?

'One million single mothers are trapped on benefits', New Labour's pre-general election manifesto informed us. Under a Labour government, the manifesto promised, lone parents would be assisted with job searches, training packages and after-school care. 'Most lone parents want to work', went the manifesto's now all-too-familiar refrain, 'but are given no help to find it'.[1]

Accordingly the 'New Deal for lone parents' was launched almost immediately the Labour government took office, swinging into action in eight test-bed locales. Lone parents with children over five, registered as unemployed and claiming benefits, were invited to contact a newly-appointed lone parent advisor who would help them to look for suitable work and help arrange childcare. Importantly, the scheme was voluntary: those lone parents who chose not to participate would retain their benefits as before. Even those who agreed to participate could drop out at any time.

Lone parents' responses to the scheme were mixed. Statistics from the Department of Social Security quoted by the *Guardian*'s David Brindle show that a total of 8,651 lone parents were invited to take part in the eight, so-called 'demonstrator' schemes. Of the 1,612 lone parents who agreed to participate, 433 found work. Put another way, just under 20 per cent of lone parents invited to take part in the scheme did so. About 27 per cent of that number got jobs. As Brindle points out: 'Whether it was a success rate of 1 in 4, or 1 in 20, was all in the eye of the beholder'.

Of course, those previously unemployed lone parents who are now working, at least part-time, as a result of the scheme, feel it has been a success for them. 'People have phoned up and been so excited (after finding work)', said one lone parent advisor based at the Benefits Agency in Sheffield. And whilst getting a job is likely to mean at least some increase in household income for lone parents, this is not the only advantage that employment has brought:

> Meeting people has meant my confidence and self-esteem has built up again. It really diminishes you if you're just stuck at home and not in contact with people. Now I am enjoying myself and no longer feel alone.[2]

But New Deal is unlikely to be a resounding success for lone parents or for the Government in the long-term. This is because the scheme does not fully address lone parents as the young women they primarily are. Instead the scheme, in principle, addresses an ungendered benefit claimant with a child. Whilst targeting particular groups might have been seen to exclude some and stigmatise others, the net effect of New Deal in its current form is precisely exclusion and stigmatisation. A few lone mothers will be able to find work of some sort through the scheme, and so join Labour's 'inclusive' society. The rest, as ever, will be left at the margins.

With the advent of New Deal, life at the margin becomes lone mothers' personal responsibility and the hard choices, a lot of government, rhetoric adds to the well-documented difficulties that lone mothers already face. Those lone mothers who choose not to participate in New Deal, and who may cite lack of affordable childcare, full-time parenting responsibilities or the uncertain benefits associated with work as reasons not to sign up, are likely to face the old cries of 'irresponsible, inadequate parent' as they do so. Harriet Harman's words at New Deal's Cambridge launch give lie to this '(F)or too long', she told lone parents, 'you have been written off to a life on benefit and then labelled as scroungers…From today, lone parents will be given a helping hand up into work, not just a hand out of benefit.'

New Deal certainly marks a change in emphasis as regards the state's view of benefit-claiming lone mothers. But at the same time it packages moral redemption as social and economic assistance and this is where its shortcomings lie, both for lone mothers themselves and for those who wish to see social divisions and economic inequalities alleviated.

The Government have cited New Deal and the recent cuts in lone parent benefit as part of their strategy to overhaul and cap welfare spending as a whole. But it is likely to find that it has got its sums wrong. New Deal and the cuts alone cannot generate the large savings that the Government hopes for, just as they cannot contribute to creating the united nation that Blair spoke of in Labour's election manifesto. Investigating the nature of the hard choices faced by lone mothers, and younger lone mothers in particular, shows why.

The economics of lone parenting

The proportion of lone parent-families to all families with children under 18 has increased since the late 1960s. With that increase has come the sense that this group constitutes something of a political and economic problem. So, what is the nature of the problem?

One answer is that in economic terms, lone parents represent a cost to the state, and by extension to the taxpayer. As the number of lone parents has increased, so has Britain's social security bill. Underlying this trend is the single most significant fact in this debate: lone parents are almost always women.

Research on lone parenting for the Department Of Social Security reports the rise in the numbers of never-married (single) lone mothers and ex-married lone mothers claiming benefits, as a proportion of all lone parents. In 1986 93 per cent of single lone mothers were claiming what was then known as 'supplementary benefit', whilst 59 per cent of ex-married lone mothers were in the same position. Bradshaw and Millar also report that: '…for single women becoming a lone mother often meant giving up regular full-time employment. At the same time, ex-married women who became lone mothers had a greater tendency to give up work than to start it, although for this group lone parenthood had less of an overall impact on employment.'[3]

Having interviewed a number of lone parents on benefits for their study, Bradshaw and Millar go on to explain that 26 per cent of them wanted to work immediately whilst a further 62 per cent wanted to work in the future. Lone mothers who didn't want to work immediately, but had hopes of future employment, gave their reasons for delaying a return to work as related to their views about the needs of their children, citing: 'the need for full-time care because the children were young or because the mother felt an extra obligation as the sole parent'.[4]

Partly as a result of the high level of benefit receipt amongst this group, lone mothers are categorically poor. A survey of UK lone parenting for the European Commission found that in 1979 about 3 in 10 lone parents had incomes less than half the average, but by 1988 this figure had risen to nearly 6 in 10.[5] When benefits are the principal income of many lone parent families, it follows that they are poor.

So why not work if, as the Government's New Deal scheme confidently proclaims, lone parents will be better off in employment?

Just over half of Bradshaw and Millar's lone parent interviewees who were claiming benefits said that they would work if appropriate and affordable childcare could be found. Furthermore a third of the women on what was then called 'income support' said that difficulties with childcare were the main or most important reason they were not working. Bradshaw and Millar report that:

> The main problem identified was cost and that working would not be worthwhile because of the cost of childcare.[6]

Reuben Ford's research for the Policy Studies Institute corroborates these findings. Asking to what extent childcare posed a barrier to work entry, he also interviewed a group of lone parents. His study found that childcare cost was the principle barrier to entry for a quarter of his subjects. He adds:

> The characteristics of these parents are typical of lone parents out of work. Hardly any received maintenance or had qualifications above 'O' level and nearly all were tenants. They were disproportionately likely to be under 25 years of age and to have a child under 11 years.[7]

These lone parents, he found, were generally unable to match the hours and rate of pay of a potential job to a childcare source they could then afford.

Ford's evidence is corroborated by Anne Phoenix's study of women who became parents whilst in their teens, *Young Mothers*. At the time the women in her study gave birth, unemployed women who were council tenants and lived alone (or with unemployed male partners) were entitled to claim supplementary benefit and had their rent paid by the DSS. If they found work, however, they lost both benefits, (although they were able to claim an in-work benefit if their incomes were low). As Phoenix points out:

> If women were to be employed...it was essential that they earned enough to pay their rents as well as (if necessary) to pay for childcare. Since most women in this study could only hope to obtain poorly paid employment they were caught in unemployment and 'poverty' traps because they could not afford to be employed.[8]

Underlying lone parents' concerns over employment and childcare costs is a segregated British labour market. Women workers are concentrated towards the bottom end of the labour market in lower-paying jobs in the catering, retail, clerical or domestic trades. Those lone parents in Bradshaw and Millar's study who worked part-time but were still eligible for income support, '...were most often in retail and catering or domestic work, they rarely worked the required hours for employment protection rights, and were not usually paying national insurance contributions'.[9] In addition the study points out that lone mothers who worked and were not on income support received pay that was lower than average female pay rates.[10]

Phoenix points out that motherhood has been shown to damage women's career prospects and lifetime earning potential in all age groups. Whilst remaining childless would enhance the earnings potential of some women, she emphasised that it would do little for those who participated in the study. Young lone mothers accounted for only some of her subjects, but it is as true for them as for young mothers with partners that: 'Had they stayed in the labour market, many ... would have experienced periods of unemployment and/or poorly paid jobs'.[11]

In short, women, who constitute the bulk of lone parents, have low earning prospects on average. This is particularly true for younger lone mothers. Paying for childcare, though, is relatively expensive and although the Childcare Disregard, (a tax break) can assist with some of these costs, it is not realisable in cash and nor are its benefits immediate. This being the case, it may appear to some lone mothers, particularly those who are young and/or lacking in qualifications or marketable skills, that staying at home to care for their children while in receipt of benefits offers the best immediate solution to their attempts to reconcile income-generation with childcare needs.

In view of this it is unsurprising that Bradshaw and Millar found income support to be very important to lone mothers. As many as 85 per cent of the women who participated in their study had received income support at some time since becoming a lone mother.[12] The 15 per cent of lone mothers who never claimed income support they found to be a distinct group consisting of previously-married, older women with school-age children. These women had educational qualifications and had tended to be employed prior to becoming lone parents:

> It seems that, for all but a distinct minority of lone mothers, receipt of income support is likely to be part of their experience of lone parenthood. The extent to which policy interventions could prevent lone mothers coming onto benefit is likely to be limited (or to require very fundamental changes). Attention should therefore be focused on helping those who want to get off benefit to be able to do so.[13]

This is the stated object of the Government's welfare-to-work scheme for lone parents claiming benefits, the New Deal.

The New Deal

The New Deal For Lone Parents was implemented in test-drive form within three months of New Labour's election victory. Launched in eight areas across England, Scotland and Wales, it is aimed at unemployed single parents with children over five years old. Crucially it is currently a voluntary scheme. Although the DSS is inviting participation from those eligible, no-one is forced to join.

Benefit claimants who are also lone parents receive a letter from their local New Deal office. Lone parents are offered advice about the benefits of work in securing 'a better future for you and your children'. If the New Deal office receives no reply, lone parents are sent a second missive reminding them of the key points in the first letter. Then they may receive a speculative visit or phone call. Those lone parents who indicate at this point that they are not interested in the scheme have no obligation to join and importantly no action is taken by the Benefits Agency against those who choose not to participate.

Those lone parents who agree to take part in New Deal set up an initial meeting with a lone parent advisor, a member of their local benefits team with special responsibility for the scheme. At that initial meeting the lone parent and her adviser consider the type of work that she might want, the type of work that is available and discuss childcare and other care issues. Next, the lone parent looks through the Benefits Agency vacancies database as well as jobhunting by other means. Subsequently, the lone parent advisor is on hand to help with writing applications and practising interview questions.

Lone parents who wish to participate in the scheme but who cannot for some reason attend an interview at the Benefits Agency can be visited by an advisor at home. Equipped with a state-of-the-art laptop and printer, the advisor can chart the jobseeking lone parent's progress and produce the much-vaunted 'better off' calculation. This calculation shows that either paid work, or a combination of paid work and in-work benefits like Family Credit, tend to generate more income than benefits alone. Lone parents can use it to judge whether or not a job is worth taking.

The 'better off' calculation is generated from details of the wage a lone parent is likely to earn if they take up a particular job for a specific number of hours. If that wage is low, the lone parent concerned may be entitled to Family Credit and Housing and Council Tax Benefit, as well as retaining Child Benefit and the first £15.00 of any child maintenance received. This income is likely to total more than benefits alone. The 'better off' calculation of a Sheffield lone parent illustrates this.

Lone parent advisors in Sheffield, where a 'demonstrator' scheme began running in July 1997, are optimistic about New Deal. Lone parents have also been receptive: 'I've been waiting for something like this for years', 'What a good idea!', 'When can I come and see you?'. And there have been results: about thirty lone parents found work through the scheme between July and October of 1997.

On closer examination the Sheffield 'New Deal' scheme reveals a more complex reality. Benefits agency staff in Sheffield estimate that approximately 3000 lone parents in the area are claiming unemployment benefits. In light of this, the fact that thirty lone parents have now found work seems less remarkable. And what forms of employment have they found? Advisors say that their clients have shown a strong

Figure 1: 'Better Off' Calculation

<u>Calculation based on your current circumstances</u>

Your current income :
You are not currently receiving any benefits.

Benefits you may be entitled to

Income Support	£80.45
Housing Benefit	£35.00
Council Tax Benefit	£7.34
Child Benefit	£26.10
Total Weekly Income:	**£148.89**

<u>Calculation based on your new/potential circumstances</u>

(working 16.00 hours per week - earning £48.00 net)

Family Credit	£79.65
Housing Benefit	£24.67
Council Tax Benefit	£4.16
Child Benefit	£26.10
Earnings	£48.00
Total Weekly Income:	**£182.58**

The difference between your weekly income:

- based on Option 1 at	**£182.58**
- and your current circumstances at	**£148.89**
=	**£33.96**

interest in, and in many cases have been pleased to take, part-time retail jobs. '(Lone parents) . . . feel excited (about work), especially if they've been out of work for a long time. One of my clients, now aged 22, hadn't worked since she left school at 16.'

But whilst lone parents are pleased to be employed, as part-time shopworkers they are likely to remain eligible for benefits, albeit in-work benefits rather than unemployment benefits. In fact, the 'better off' calculation reproduced above was derived from the circumstances of a real Sheffield lone parent who was considering part-time work, in a particular retail job, and who planned to leave her child with a relative if she took up employment.

A swathe of lone parents employed in low-paid, part-time work that needs topping up with in-work benefits will not allow the Government to save much on welfare expenditure. The cost of assistance will simply become the responsibility of a different set of budgets within departmental purses. But the Government scores a political victory when lone mothers are working, being able to claim that those lone mothers subscribe to the shared values and purpose – in this case, a work ethic – of which Blair speaks in Labour's election manifesto. Work is the better way, Joan Ruddock MP, Minister For Women, argued, at a meeting hosted by Islington Council to promote the Government's plans for women.

Do the lone mothers who have chosen not to participate in New Deal also think that work is the better way? Possibly so, but with labour market opportunities limited for those with few marketable skills and little recent work experience, many who have not worked of late will have little hope of finding employment that appears to be worth upsetting their current balance of domestic and pecuniary arrangements. At the same time, some of those lone mothers who rang benefits offices to find out what sanctions might be set in motion of they did not join, have been persuaded by the scheme, on finding participation to be voluntary.

Sheffield advisors received a number of such calls from lone mothers concerned that their benefits might be stopped if they did not participate in the scheme. They found lone mothers were often surprised to hear that no sanctions would be deployed if they chose not to register. 'Lone parents have found it hard to accept that the Benefits Agency are actually doing something for them and not saying they've got to do it', commented one advisor. They think the absence of sanctions has made New Deal more attractive to some of the initially reluctant or hesitant. 'We're not forcing anybody', 'I think that makes (lone parents) want to do it more. They're doing it because they want to not because they have to'.

But the *Guardian*'s David Brindle has warned that enthusiasm for the scheme will last only as long as it is voluntary and there are deep suspicions, he says, that voluntary status will not last. Ministers may, for example, be considering 'an availability for work' test when a lone parent's youngest child starts their second term at primary school.

Harriet Harman has assured us that there will be no compulsion for lone mothers to work.[14] She has also announced Lottery-funded childcare intended to assist those who want to work and can find employment. But she has made it clear, too, that her departmental policy initiatives be far-removed from an old-style socialism that would tackle the poverty and social exclusion experienced by some lone mothers and a number of other groups via 'tax and spend'. Instead she says, 'We will tackle (poverty and social exclusion) by welfare to work, encouraging savings and reforming the welfare state'.[15]

Harman's remarks reflect the new-style so-called 'ethical socialism' of Blair and his supporters. Beatrix Campbell, for one, has commented on what she calls '...a swing away from ideology and back to ethics' within the Labour Party. She links this to the influence of communitarian ideas among Labour's policy makers.[16] But the underlying communitarianism of policy initiatives like New Deal mean that any pretensions to enhancing social and economic equalities that they may have are negated in the act of implementation.

Blair in the community

Some of Labour's communitarian-inspired vision is derived from the popular communitarianism of US political scientist Amatai Etzioni. His book *The Spirit Of Community* (1995) argues that '. . . communities constantly need to be pulled towards the centre course, where individual rights and social responsibilities are properly balanced'. *The Spirit of Community*, it might be said, adds a 1990s gloss to the age-old tension between the claims made by liberals for autonomy and individual freedoms, and a perceived necessity for constraints on those freedoms in certain circumstances. This means it has been eagerly set upon by New Labour who have been keen to move away from socialist-derived, ideologically-informed statism, while retaining the ability to effect some sort of social, economic and political change en masse.

New Labour appears to recognise that real social and economic inequalities currently exist: 'There is a wider gap between rich and poor than for generations. . .' said their manifesto. 'There are over one million fewer jobs in Britain than in 1990'.[17] But a communitarian-inspired Labour's solutions to Britain's social and economic problems do not lie with wealth redistribution. Instead Blair et al propound a revised version of the Protestant work ethic they call 'stakeholding'. This, they equate with 'community' participation.

In a stakeholder economy, says Labour, '...everyone has a stake in society and owes responsibilities to it'.[18] Existing inequalities mean, though, that some, through no fault of their own, currently have no stakes. Cue initiatives like New Deal which represent Labour's attempt to distribute stakes to those who, in their view, have been stakeless. But those who do not take the proferred stakes are made culpable. 'The unemployed have a responsibility to take up the opportunity of training places or work…' says Labour.[19] Proper adherence to one's responsibilities as a citizen of New Britain contributes to the maintenance of 'strong communities'. This is only as much as Britons already desire, say Labour.[20] But will strengthened communities lead to greater equality for currently disadvantaged groups?

In fact, 'community' and 'equality' are not coterminous. Moreover, any notion of change affiliated to a 'politics of community' can be shown to contradict and undermine the very principles of equality New Labour professes to support. The 'communitarianism' which inspires that politics, as Elizabeth Frazer and Nicola Lacey (1993) have pointed out:

> … is flawed by a conception of the self and of society which is incapable of explicating radical politics … [I]t turns out to be potentially conservative, as well as sharing with modern liberal theory a lack of attention to gender and the absence of a theory of power.[21]

In short, a communitarian-informed politics pronounces a moral imperative for, rather than a political incitement to, change.

New Deal clearly works in just this way. The scheme conceives the tension between labour market participation and parenting responsibilities as a problem to be solved via an appeal to 'right and wrong'. 'You can be better off in work' exclaims the slogan on the cover of the New Deal Action Pack, given to lone parents participating in the scheme, whilst lone parents' New Deal invitation letters tell them 'Getting a job really does offer a better future for you and your children. . .'.

In this vein, Marie Fields, herself a lone mother, and employed by New Deal after eight years out of work to sell the scheme to others in the same boat, told the *Guardian*:

> '. . . I've got a job, my kids see me going to work, they're going to grow up with the work ethic'.[22]

But what of those who cannot or do not choose to find work? Affordable childcare and job opportunities aside, such enthusiastic endorsement of work for lone mothers is a very recent development. As Jane Lewis points out, Conservatives have traditionally been ambivalent about whether to encourage mothers to work outside the home.[23] It has been Conservative rhetoric which younger lone mothers will have grown up with. It is difficult to blame women for wanting to stay at home with young children if they have previously understood this to be the 'right' choice. It is even more difficult to blame them if staying at home, or at least not working on a full-time basis, would still appear to be the 'right' choice for women with partners. Lone mother Alison Hogg believed that even though New Deal had helped her find work, '. . . if I had another child I would want to stay at home until they were five'.[24]

Hogg's words reveal what, now more than ever, are conflicting obligations for lone mothers. First, parents are obliged to care for their children. In fact, they have a legal duty to do so, although most would feel their obligation rather differently – conceiving their responsibility as primarily due to their family and to the child itself. New Deal formalises further obligations – to the labour market, to the state, and to the 'community'. These sets of obligations are in competition. Some lone parents who have access to affordable childcare or who have highly marketable skills are able to effect a compromise between them. Others choose to remain at home until they feel their child is of an age that will allow them to work. Still others would like to work but recognise that the low paid part-time work they are likely to find, alongside the affordable childcare that is hard to come by, means that fulfilling their obligation to the labour market will disproportionately disrupt the fulfilment of their domestic obligations.

These two latter groups are the lone parents that New Deal aims to 'help', by restating their obligation to work. But New Deal employee Marie Fields' words indicate that the proffered 'help' is not all it seems. 'I don't think anyone's entitled to anything', . . . 'If you're out of work, you're not entitled to sit at home, smoke fags and watch Neighbours'. Her view is resonant with recent New Right thinking on welfare. US academic Lawrence Mead has spoken of the 'remoralisation' of those claiming welfare benefits, suggesting that automatic citizen rights (to benefits, for example) be replaced by an obligation to work in exchange for assistance.[25] In addition, as Jane Lewis points out, other New Right theorists have suggested that it is better for a child to have a breadwinner mother than no 'example' at all.[26]

New Labour communitarianism, it seems, shares some territory with the New Right ideas more beloved of Thatcherism. Both address the question of rights, although communitarianism packages rights with responsibilities while New Right thinking suggests that there is no automatic relationship between the two. But recognising the New

Right agenda that lies quietly to one side of Labour's 'politics of community' unmasks a threat to those who do not wish to or cannot participate in their 'communities' on Labour's terms.

The threat is one of social and economic exclusion from New Labour's inclusive society. Those unemployed lone mothers who wish to join the club must address their circumstances and transform them, via labour market participation, as a condition of entry. The principal carrot offered to them is the promise of better social and economic conditions – an aspiration to 'equality' – whilst the stick is not sanctions (Frank Field MP, Harriet Harman's deputy said that he saw no point in sanctions) 'equality' is denied.

Unemployed lone mothers, and others targeted by the Government's welfare reforms, can take one step nearer 'equality' as they are assimilated into the workforce: if they have found suitable work and affordable childcare they are likely to be in pocket to some degree and they can also bask in their raised 'community' approval rating. But the process of alleviating inequalities in New Britain is as much about individual lone mothers subscribing to 'correct' cultural values as it is about righting an imbalance of power between different social and economic groups.

This being so, younger unemployed lone mothers – never married, with few qualifications or marketable skills and a limited prospect of finding childcare at a price which matches the low-paid part-time work available to them – will continue to be seen as the 'scroungers' of popular myth, in contrast to those who have found suitable work and affordable childcare and 'grown up' into the responsible citizens of the New Labour model.

In effect, then, the New Deal For Lone Parents, is just the same old hat for those it is attempting to reach. 'Correct' values are immaterial for lone mothers – especially younger mothers – who cannot find work that will make it worth leaving their child for long periods. New Deal's recipe, communitarianism with a hint of New Right, cannot nourish those it is intended to feed. It only satisfies those who write the menus.

Notes

1. The Labour Party, *New Labour: Because Britain Deserves Better*, election manifesto, Labour Party, London 1997, p19.
2. Interview with Alison Hogg, a lone parent who found employment

through the scheme in, S. Hall, 'Mother's First Job Hope in 16 Years' *The Guardian*, 31 December 1997.

3. J. Bradshaw and J. Millar, *Lone Parent Families in the UK*, DSS Research Report No.6, HMSO, London 1991, p96.

4. *Ibid.*

5. J. Millar, 'Lone Parent Families in the European Community: UK', in J. Roll (ed), *Lone Parent Families in the European Community: A Report to the European Commission*, European Families and Social Policy Unit, London 1992, p33.

6. Bradshaw and Millar, *op.cit.*, p96.

7. R. Ford, *Childcare In the Balance: How Lone Parents Make Decisions About Work*, Policy Studies Institute, London 1996, p202.

8. A. Phoenix, *Young Mothers?*, Polity, Cambridge 1991, p220.

9. Bradshaw and Millar, *op.cit.*, p96.

10. *Ibid.*

11. Phoenix, *op.cit.*, p221.

12. Bradshaw and Millar, *op.cit.*, p97.

13. *Ibid.*

14. S. Richards, 'Interview: Harriet Harman, *New Statesman*, 28 November 1997.

15. *Ibid.*

16. B. Campbell, 'Old Fogeys and Young Men: A Critique of Communitarianism', *Soundings*, Issue 1, Lawrence & Wishart, 1995.

17. The Labour Party, *op.cit.*, p19.

18. *Ibid.*

19. *Ibid.*

20. *Ibid.*

21. E. Frazer and N. Lacey, *The Politics of Community*, Harvester Wheatsheaf, 1993, p163.

22. Interview with Marie Fields, A. Perkins, 'I've got a job, my kids see me going to work. . .', *The Guardian*, 15 January 1998.

23. J. Lewis, 'Lone Mothers: The British Case, in J. Lewis (ed) *Lone Mothers in European Welfare Regimes: Shifting Policy Logics*, Jessica Kingsley, London 1992, p66.

24. S. Hall, *op.cit.*

25. L. Mead, *Beyond Entitlement*, The Free Press, New Yale 1986.

26. Lewis, *op.cit.*

Contributors

Jonathan Rutherford is part of the Sign of the Times group and his latest book is *Forever England: Reflections on Masculinity and Empire*, Lawrence & Wishart, 1997. He is a Lecturer in Cultural Studies at Middlesex University.

Noshin Ahmad is a freelance writer.

Ian Brinkley is a TUC researcher.

Balbir Chatrik is Director of Youth Aid, which is a charity working on issues of youth unemployment.

Peter Gartside is a freelance writer.

Frances O'Grady is the director of the TUC's New Unionism Campaign.

Rupa Huq is a PhD student at the University of East London.

Jonathan Keane is a freelance journalist and broadcaster.

Michael Kenny is Lecturer in Politics at Sheffield University, currently a visiting lecturer at William and Mary College, USA.

Bilkis Malek is researching South Asian film/video cultures at Middlesex University and British Film Institute.

Elaine Pennicott is a PhD student at Middlesex University

Karen Triggs is a freelance writer.